BE THE ORCA

A MENOPAUSE MANIFESTO

BE THE ORCA

A MENOPAUSE MANIFESTO

AMY EIR STOCKY

PATINA PRESS
WEHAVEPATINA.COM
©2024

Be The Orca: A Menopause Manifesto
Copyright © 2024 by Amy Eir Stocky
Patina Press - wehavepatina.com

All Right Reserved. No part of this publication may be reproduced or transmitted in any form, or by any means, electronic or mechanical, including photocopying, or recording, or by any information storage and retrieval system, without permission in writing from Amy Eir Stocky and/or The Patina Press
2733 SE 84th Place, Portland OR 97266.
Thank you for supporting small press and independent publishers.
Thank you for honoring this copyright.

Print Edition ISBN: 978-1-7367759-2-9
E-Book Edition ISBN: 978-1-7367759-3-6

Cover painting by Ryan Case

Design and layout by Amy Eir Stocky
Editorial assistance: Amelia Lamb

FOR ALL MY SISTERS ACROSS THE WORLD, WE ARE ONE.

"We're all going to die, all of us, what a circus!
That alone should make us love each other but it doesn't.
We are terrorized and flattened by trivialities;
we are eaten up by nothing."

~ Charles Bukowski

BE THE ORCA

A MENOPAUSE MANIFESTO

AMY EiR STOCKY

PATiNA PRESS
WEHAVEPATINA.COM
COPYRIGHT©2024 AMY EiR STOCKY

BE THE ORCA

CONTENTS

WELCOME! ____ 11

WHY BE AN ORCA? ____ 12

SURVIVING MENOPAUSE: MY STORY ____ 13

HOW TURNING 50 BECAME MAYBE THE BEST TIME IN MY LIFE... ____ 16

WE ARE THE "NEW OLD"! ____ 18

TAKE THE REINS ____ 19

WHAT IS LEFT ON YOUR LIST? ____ 22

FORGETTING OUR POWER... NO MORE! ____ 24
  WHERE CAN WE STAND? WILL YOU HOLD MY HAND?
  WHAT COULD WE DO TOGETHER?

AGING IS A CRIME, AND OTHER MYTHICAL BS ____ 31
  BEING A WOMAN IS A MISDEMEANOR

BAD HISTORICAL PRECEDENCE ____ 34

THE STRANGER IN THE MIRROR ____ 35

GEODES AND AGING ____ 38

MY IRRATIONAL FEAR OF THE INDEPENDENT WOMEN OF ASTORIA ____ 40

TAKING CARE OF VESSELS, OR ONLY FLOSS THE ONES YOU WANT TO KEEP ____ 42

THE END OF THE PERIOD ____ 48

HOT FLASHES & OTHER EXCITEMENT ____ 51
  TO ESTROGEN OR NOT TO ESTROGEN? THAT IS THE QUESTION

SEX AND MENOPAUSE 57
  LOVE YOURSELF! SELF-PLEASURE IS BEAUTIFUL
  DON'T FAKE IT TIL YOU MAKE IT

EMOTIONAL OUTBURSTS 64

SECURITY IS A HOAX 67
  FEAR OF CHANGE, SECURITY, AND OUR PATH

WHAT IS A SUCCESSFUL RELATIONSHIP? 75
  CONFLICT HAPPENS IN ALL RELATIONSHIPS
  A BRIEF ON FRIENDSHIP
  FRENEMIES
  DO YOU LOVE YOURSELF?

SHADOW SIDE WORKOUT: FOR A FUTURE WITHOUT CHAINS 85
  HAPPINESS IS AN INSIDE JOB
  BACK TO THAT DEBT THING
  FUCK FRENEMIES, ALL WOMEN ARE SISTERS
  IT'S TIME TO WORK OUT YOUR DARK SIDE
  LEARNING OUR BOUNDARIES
  GENERATIONAL TRAUMA
  EXPERIENTIAL TRAUMA
  HEALING AND CARING FOR OUR INNER CHILD
  TRICKS OF THE EGO
  OVERCOMING SOCIETAL BULLSHIT

CONTROLLING OUTCOMES 102

MAKE NO TIME FOR REGRET 104

EXPECTATION IS THE KILLER OF JOY 106

WORRY IS A FAILED STATE 108

UNIVERSE EXPERIMENTS 109

SURVIVING OLD AGE IN A STRANGE WORLD -- OR WHERE ARE YOU HUNKERING DOWN? _____ 112

IDLE HANDS = BRAIN DEATH _____ 117

THE FREEDOM OF TODAY - WE ARE LIMITLESS! _____ 123
   NO COMPROMISE

IT'S THE 4TH QUARTER, IMAGINE YOUR PERFECT LIFE _____ 126
   WHAT IS YOUR PERFECT LIFE?

A LITTLE SELF-CARE INTERLUDE... _____ 132

FOR THE FOURTH QUARTER PLANNING IS IMPORTANT _____ 133

WRITE YOUR OBITUARY _____ 135

IMMORTALITY _____ 137

MAKE YOUR WILL, BUT MAKE YOUR WILL _____ 140
   PREP TALK PEP TALK - WHAT IS YOUR WILL?

DEATH COMES FOR US ALL _____ 143
   BEYOND DEATH

GRIEF IS EXHAUSTING _____ 146

ONLY AS STRONG AS THE WEAKEST DECKHAND _____ 149

FOR THE MEN IN OUR LIVES: CHANGING FROM THE WARRIOR TO THE SHAMAN, WISE MAN, OR CHIEF _____ 151

ARE YOU LEAVING MORE THAN JUST A STAIN? _____ 153

IN CONCLUSION _____ 162

WELCOME!

I've tried to make this beneficial for anyone who might pick it up, but truly it is for you, my sisters in menopause. If you are going through, have gone through, or will go through the mysterious chapter in our lives known as menopause, this little book will hopefully offer courage and encouragement to you. This is a remarkable time, so forget the fear and don't believe the hype.

It seems most people see menopause as something bad. Something not to be discussed. Old age (older age in general) is spooky territory. It doesn't have to be. What if we embrace it? Menopause is just another amazing stage in life and there's no reason to approach it with apprehension. There's also no reason to count ourselves out.

When I began to document my thoughts and experiences regarding aging, I had no idea what if anything it would become. They were just little essays, rants, or epiphanies I'd have and write in a notebook or type on my computer. I'd been just sticking the writings in a folder on my computer. One day I opened the folder and found I had quite a lot of stuff written on this subject.

I realize these essays and rants are really pep talks for myself, but I share them to maybe help others benefit from my experiences. I wish for them to serve not just menopausal women, but anyone experiencing changes in their life, or those wanting to better understand a woman's final cycle.

The universe kept pushing, giving me little signs and nudges, saying I HAD to release this manifesto until I could no longer deny it. As I started searching through and transcribing from my notebooks, I was surprised the essays went back over two years.

Some subjects I wrote about more than once even, which I have to admit has been the most difficult aspect of editing this project. In some instances the point or perspective was similar; in others, wildly different. Some things might seem redundant - maybe we need to hear it twice? I don't feel any ego about it, nor any shame.

It is far from a perfect effort. There is more I wanted to say, or I'd like to have said better but so it goes, and here it is. I hope you find this helpful, and that it encourages you to lean into becoming the Orca!

WHY BE AN ORCA?

'Be the Orca' came to me after reading an article about how Orcas, aka Killer Whales, are one of very few animals to go through menopause, and it is the menopausal females who lead the pods. I am not calling us menopausal ladies whales... Well I guess I am, but not in any derogatory way. It is meant as an honor, a call to action, perhaps even a call to arms.

Study is showing that other primates and elephants likely have a similar experience, which makes perfect sense, but little is known about primate menopause. Study of the natural world around us is meager in this era of arrogance, and the study of women's health is stunningly minimal. Some might say both are criminally absent from real research. We are partially to blame, we barely speak about our womanly cycles and almost no one talks about their menopause. I say no more!

This project isn't about science so much, it's more philosophical, a manifesto if you will. It's about righting some fundamental flaws in our thinking as a society. Consider it an alternative view on aging, a "new" old.

It's not merely that the Orca has menopause, it's about that second part of the statement - that the menopausal females lead the pods. Lead. The. Pod. What a concept, especially in America where we earn seventy cents to the dollar of our male counterparts in jobs still today! WTF. Perhaps this is the problem in the western world, our inequality is destroying us?

It's time to take our rightful place and fix this mess! First, we need to heal ourselves or we can't help our legacy or the world. We need to be able to stand strong! This is a time to shine and not shame at who we are, and who we are becoming.

When I started this manifesto with the concept of 'Be the Orca', it was some months before Orcas were first reported to be swimming around knocking over yachts. The news of those remarkable events seemed like a certain sign to continue forward, and so I have. They have too!

Now, I invite you on this little journey with me. Please come along and let's turn this upside-down world into the paradise it could be for all of us, for all of the beings on this glorious place we call Earth, and in this exciting moment we call our lifetime. This time is a gift! Let us use it to create a new world around us, and a better day for all! Be the Orca!

SURVIVING MENOPAUSE: MY STORY

It's weird, no one talks about menopause, right? Really bizarre. My mother said one day that her period had stopped and she was happy about it. That was all she ever said about her experience.

In my life, I haven't had many female friends. The older ladies I knew spoke of other health issues like cancer or obesity. Menopause wasn't seeming to be on their radar at all. Maybe a passing comment on hot flashes.

So when my period became seasonal more than monthly, I knew something was happening, but I had no idea what I was really getting into. It has not been a bad experience so far, just another thing to marvel at. My final period thus far was Spring Equinox 2021. I buried the last tampon I used in the yard. Seemed kind of sacred so I did it. It wasn't anything I'd read.

Thus I began my inevitable quest to follow this experience along. I have been pretty open about it with friends and lovers, and I have found that the mere mention of menopause got people really curious and wanting to know more. It is such a strangely taboo subject. Why? Why don't we talk about it? I had to give that a lot of thought. I've pondered it a while now, and it appears to be a lot of things, from societal fear of the aged and our shallow youth focused culture, to our own fears of death and how we feel about ourselves.

There was a lot to consider and questions left unanswered by research. Many women choose to take estrogen to keep from entering menopause. Why did they do that? Was I gonna gain 50 pounds and become a troll woman with a beard? Would I lose my sex drive? I was a little concerned.

Social media's unbelievably knowledgeable algorithm began serving me all these ads for face creams, face lifts, diet apps, and so much more. What the hell did I look up? Or did my saver card at the grocery store alert the socials that I haven't bought tampons in a while? I'm not sure. Who knows these days?

Anyway, I started taking notes, doing research, and observing. I combined mushrooms with meditations, and paired it with my decades of ponderous research on a variety of related or referenced topics, and I've come up with my own views on this whole thing. In this small tome, I have tried to cover the myriad of topics related to this whole menopause experience, and how to make the most of our time before we leave these fleshy bodies.

At this point in life, we've all had a lot of experiences. Perhaps multiple careers, kids, marriages. We've had triumphs and heartbreaks. I mean, we got here, to this age. Not everyone makes it. We've seen a lot, and there have certainly been some bumps and bruises...

My own start toward menopause was filled with unexpected change in my personal life. Namely, the sudden and shocking end of my 20-some year marriage. The whole terrible crash of it hit like a meteor and left a crater that took five years with it. The emotional toll and the work I had to do personally to free myself, not just legally but emotionally and mentally, has been an all uphill hike so far. I've endured a years long divorce, nearly five years of nonsense, harassment, cyber attacks and bullying, defamation even.

I never thought my marriage would end, let alone like that! The marriage itself was tumultuous and our lives constantly unsettled by circumstance. In retrospect, I guess it should not have been such a surprise, but I was totally shocked and devastated when my husband left in the middle of the night filled with anger and fear.

We were often creative or business partners on projects. We were best friends! Together we made a lot of stuff, we had a lot of adventures, and now this person was my worst enemy. For what reason I knew not, nothing made sense. It was all so crazy.

That happened in early January, 2019. I have written much about it privately, to share it "in brief" here has been really difficult. I've written and rewritten various explanations multiple times in trying to offer some brief account, but it becomes too stressful to think about. It's overwhelming. The previous few paragraphs are the best I can muster.

Why it's important is this, in the process of that heartbreak, in all the pain and change and grief, I came to love myself. A whole new world opened up to me. As I stood on the precipice, things could have gone a lot of ways. I needed to thrive and not just live through it. There was no going back, so I marched forward.

"Soldier on." My sister said. I have found so much wonder and wisdom in the years since then, but at the time, I never thought I'd survive it.

Everything I thought about my life and my future was suddenly different. Now I had to navigate this new life alone at 49. How would I manage? How had I gotten there? There was so much grief over the breakup I needed to process. Plus, a full-time job I'd been at for only two months. Plus, a house I bought just a year earlier that was four months behind on the mortgage and facing foreclosure. Talk about being a ball of stress and worry. I was desperate for relief, I needed understanding and purpose.

I needed help fast so I started doing yoga on YouTube. In his mountainous book, 'The Body Keeps The Score', Bessel van der Kolk suggests that yoga is one of the best ways to process trauma and release it from the body. I thought that was a good place to start. I searched around and then happened upon 'Yoga with Adrienne', on YouTube. Her sweet demeanor was just the gentle encouragement I needed. I did the yoga video classes for stress, for digestion, and shorter ones to start. I still do yoga with her videos today.

I walked my dog more and more, getting out into the forest or the parks as much as we could, taking in the neighborhoods, and exploring by car. I began meditating, or trying anyway. I went to a good therapist. I did so many things to process and try to grow from the experience.

I share this here to explain where I am coming from. If I make some reference, as I do in some of the essays, you the reader won't be in the dark. The less I mention it the better, but if it is relevant in some way to some point I am making I may mention it. I apologize in advance for redundancy or trauma tangents. I'm trying to offer some context, that's all.

I didn't know how I would ever get through the end of my marriage, but I did. And then I got through the Pandemic. I wrote and made art and healed. It was hard - I had to consider many painful truths and shake off a lot of trauma.

For me, the last five years were so emotionally heavy with heartbreak and healing, an amazing rediscovery of My Self, and building a new life, that when the whole menopause thing did start it was not really a cross to bear. It was perhaps the easiest part of the last five years, which is not to minimize it in any way. It has been a big part of my journey.

This is a big deal, this menopause. The biggest question being why hide it? Why not make it a celebration? That is what I hope to encourage here - a celebration of this time, of this part of womanhood, and our lives in general as the big event it is!

HOW TURNING 50 BECAME MAYBE THE BEST TIME IN MY LIFE...

As I look back over my life, it really shouldn't be surprising that these recent years have been some of my best. In this modern American society, there is a lot of focus on growing up and setting up our lives in our 20s, 30s, and 40s. Now in my 50s, the die has been cast, meaning I am this person my experiences, pursuits, and interests have made me. Far from broken, I feel given my past experiences I can achieve anything now!

The question is, what is "anything"? What are my desires? My true desires, and my will? It is great to realize at this age, an age that at 25 I would have imagined to be the "duller" phase in my life, it is actually more rich and exquisite in its beauty than any so far.

Of course I have had my share of hardships. I've lost both my parents at this point, and had a twenty-some year marriage end in disaster. I've moved maybe 20 times in the last 30 years or so. I've lost a lot and gained a lot over the years. I've succeeded and I have failed. I've failed spectacularly sometimes, and I've been down, so down, and I've felt alone. Those are the things that make life precious. When we know how bad things can be, we appreciate every period of good tidings and we relish every moment of magic.

I seldom think of any of the misfortunes or bad times in my life. When they come up in a re-visit of history, or some storytelling, they just are what they are. Moments in the past, things I've grown from, some I wear the scars of.

I have a soft perspective on life. I am forgiving and compassionate. I am lighthearted most of the time, and I am great in an emergency - because I've been in enough of them! I've seen the most beautiful sunrises and sunsets and starry night skies I ever could have imagined! I've seen miracles and magic moments galore, I've celebrated amazing achievements of those around me and my own, and I have smelled a million flowers! My life is filled with joy as far as I am concerned. The bad times are few and the good times so many. Some might argue with me on that, but again, it all comes down to perspective.

I never would have imagined at 20, 30, or even 40 that turning 50, especially during one of the hardest moments of my life, would become the exciting new beginning it is! A rebirth of everything about myself! It has offered me so many beautiful moments I never would have experienced had that tragic event not occurred!

Since my marriage imploded, I've experienced so much growth! I have developed my independence. I've dated and experienced new lovers for the first time since my 20s. That has been a delight beyond my imagination. I made mistakes in some of the relationships I got myself entangled in, and realized I was pretty naive about how to navigate romance. But the universe has brought a handful of amazing people into my life. And for that I have no regrets. Few, anyway.

The fact is, I could have looked at this experience in a lot of ways, I could have focused on the heartbreak and never dated again. I could have grown bitter or jaded, or become overly promiscuous. I chose instead to embrace whatever was coming my way. I would try to be kind to myself and not self-destructive. I decided if I looked toward the best, and did my best, the best would come.

For me, I am celebrating many freedoms that would be hard to explain. I am responsible for me now, only me. I rise or fall based solely on me. There is a comfort in partnership, but at this moment the universe says I need to go it alone, and I am heeding that. It's what is right for me. What's right for you is right for you. Partnership is a beautiful thing. Maybe I will get there again some day.

My next order of business is learning to stand tall, fully on my own, on my path. I now accept that instead of struggling to survive, it is okay to thrive! I have overcome my fear of failure, but even more, my fear of success. Now I am open to life.

WE ARE THE "NEW OLD"!

It's easy for me to comfort someone who is grieving because I have experienced my share of grief. I tell them, "grief is exhausting", and I urge them to be easy on themselves, and sleep when they need to because grief takes so much energy. I delight in passing wisdom on. I have knowledge to share. To say I see you, I understand, I'm here. That feels good to me. It feels like what I am supposed to do.

That experience is a great thing to have, yet when I look at photos of my grandmother at what must be close to my age, I don't relate. I don't feel I'm ready for a house dress. I look at friends my age, across real life and social media, and none of us seem ready for grandma shoes, even the ones who are in fact grandmas. We are different. We are not the 50+ of fifty years ago. This gives us a new opportunity.

Years ago I watched Bettie Davis play an old woman in a horror movie. In looking it up online, I found out she was barely 36 at the time. Further research revealed in the 1950s and '60s an actress near 40 years of age was relegated to grandma roles. Today, we have 50-year-olds playing teenagers, as so many jokes report. Something has happened with our generation and those younger where age is much more relative. Sure, it's probably all the preservatives we ate as kids, but so it is.

Since we have this different time before us, we should capitalize on it! I'm going to do all I can before the lounge-wear forever days are upon me, or I'm bedridden, or whatever eventually takes me out takes hold. One of my strong points is my ability to enjoy the moment and make the best of every situation. I can "have fun in a paper bag", as they say. There are beautiful moments around us all the time if we just open our eyes. A sunbeam, the glow of the moon, a kind gesture, a willingness to try, all of it beautiful in its own way.

I try to appreciate every single day. We need to savor every moment we have now, and celebrate every day we wake up. I really want to get this project out for whatever reason. You have something you wish to do for whatever reason. If we step away from the meaningless nonsense cluttering up our lives and step into what is really important to us, we can make this time in our lives really spectacular.

If you are an accountant, how can you use your skills and knowledge to help our fellow man, animal, tree, drop of water? If you are a berry picker how can you share your knowledge to make life better? None of us is better than the other, and none of us are here without each other. We all have important knowledge and skills to share.

I learned from the history of a fishing town on the mouth of the Columbia River about the Swedish fishermen who in the 1880s built a network of union canneries along the river's edge. They created for themselves on their terms, fair prices, fair wages, and decent working conditions, it became a model for others. They lived by the belief that "work is our joy!". Right, work is our joy? Is it? It should be joy. If it isn't, why isn't it? Perhaps "right work" is our joy. I don't mean that grandiosely, I'm speaking of fishermen. Humble but honorable fishermen have fed communities since time immemorial.

A sense of purpose is everything in finding our joy. I decided in this rebirth of me, this totally different life on my own, I will put forth what I was born to do. As hard as it was, it has birthed this amazing new period of my life, one I never anticipated!

We are not ready to go gently into that good night. Maybe someday I will wake up with a wild urge to rock in a chair and crochet, (not that crocheting or rocking chairs are necessarily age specific), but I feel still full of energy, full of life, strong and vital! I feel sharp mentally. I have healed much of my generational trauma and my personal trauma. I have worked hard to understand myself and what I really want and need.

What could I do? I am sharing my philosophy and these beliefs in an effort to unite us in ways we should be united, to empower us in ways we should be empowered. It's the old 'leave it better than you found it' feeling. This is my current attempt at that, to help others maneuver this dazzling moment of our life, this amazing next part - The Big Finale!!!

TAKE THE REiNS

Take the reins, your own reins, take them back. We are no longer beasts of burden to society. One of my most freeing moments was the realization that in society's view of me as an older woman, I was now useless, invisible, and only supposed to appear on cue with a plate of gingerbread men. Instead of making me feel sadness or longing. However, it had the opposite effect. This brand new obsolescence gave me the freedom to do anything I wanted, to be anyone I wanted.

I was, in a word, limitless! There were no obligations, there were no more traditions I needed to honor or follow. I was a free agent. While being "invisible" can be hard, it is also fun!

Now that is not to say I'm living some high life, retired with a pension (what's that?), or anything of that nature. Few of us get to experience retirement like we've been sold. I'm still working, I am still struggling, probably until I drop. This is about our mindset and our focus, and taking control of it.

Sometimes our jobs have been mundane. Some of our lives have been a wild ride and we are unapologetic for it. No two of us are the same, so this will be different for each of us. This is the time when no one else's view matters anymore. Maybe I am just saying this for myself to hear, well I mean indeed I am. Now is the time I stop letting life happen to me.

Not to say I don't have accomplishments I am proud of. It's just that time is running out and I have so much more I still want to do. I need to think strategically about it. Every single day counts - none of us knows when our number is up.

Since I was a child I always had a keen interest in the occult, science and magic. It just makes sense that we are moving energy, as are our thoughts and actions. We are energy. We are all part of the same energy. Everyone is our brethren. Everything on this planet is part of us. Love and our own life force are the same energy. When I learned about neutrinos in a physics lab at the bottom of an old ore mine, these tiny invisible energy particles all around us, and that we can direct with our thoughts and actions, I knew magic was real. I believe that is where our personal power lives, in the ability to focus those tiny neutrinos at our goals, our real goals whatever they are. Do we even know? Do we scatter our energy so much we dissipate it?

We've done all the things to make our parents happy, or unhappy as the case may have been for the rebels out there. We've probably partnered up, maybe multiple times, and tried to please our mates. If we had kids, we did the whole child rearing thing, however rewarding and/or thankless that turned out.

We've served employers, maybe not at our dream jobs, but the best we could do to meet our basic needs and hopefully more. We've been consumers, some more than others. We've done all kinds of stuff, for better or worse, to fit into whatever mold society has given us, or that we have reached out and grabbed.

Some of us appear to be living the high life, or it could be an illusion built on insurmountable debt. Some of us live simply by choice or by fate. It has never mattered less.

Here is where we stop serving others. We must serve ourselves from here on out. Life is uncertain. We cannot wait for permission any longer, we can no longer leave any leftover dreams and goals to fate. Put yourself back into the animal kingdom for a moment, even just your backyard birds and squirrels. They could be having the best day ever, then a dog or cat grabs them from behind. When they say 'bad things happen to good people', perhaps we can rephrase it to merely 'bad things happen'.

These days are limitless but limited. Show the world your loving kindness, emulate all the character traits you wish to live by. Because tomorrow has no guarantees - Take the reins of your life. Because we have so much still to offer the world - Take the reins!

Have you always been unreliable, and now you see it in your kids and loathe it? Have you always been a goody two shoes and now you realize you forgot to live? Are you an armchair activist with strong views but never the time to actually stand for what you believe in service? This is all fixable!

Stop waiting for things to happen for you and make them happen the way you want them to. If you've been a grocery store clerk, but you were always fascinated with welding or mechanics, make a leap! If it's second, third, or fourth career time, make that jump! If you're self-employed or an artist maybe try something different, or go all in as never before. Taking the reins of our destiny, to make conscious decisions to serve our ultimate goals, our dreams, our what-ifs, is what this time is about! We are not stuck to the rules of the past, or of society, and thank goodness, because the wheels are coming off that ride! Now is the time! We have to truly take the reins, lead our pod, and push forward.

WHAT IS LEFT ON YOUR LIST?

I'm going to ask you right now, take a moment to consider all of the dreams you had for yourself at different points in life. What were your goals at 24? Or at 42? How did those go? How did they change?

This isn't about shaming anyone. On the contrary, I offer sincere congratulations that you made it this far. It doesn't matter if you are reading this in a mansion, an apartment, or a prison cell. At this point we understand a couple of things: No one is all good or all bad. Nothing is black and white. Relationships are complex.

Despite whatever hand we were dealt in regard to our family, our communities and surroundings, and our luck or misfortune, we have somehow managed to make it to this age! The age of menopause! Many people never make it here, so give yourself a warm hug, a generous pat on the back, whatever you feel comfortable with. This isn't sarcasm.

Try looking back at your life objectively and appreciating your successes and celebrations, and all the hardships you endured and survived. I bet there were some wonderful twists and turns? There were for me too! My life so far has been a roller coaster, and while I did achieve many goals in different ways, I am also not where I expected to be in life. I've really struggled. But that happens in this mutated world of chasing dollars rather than doing what we were born for.

> How did you imagine your life turning out when you were 12? What did you want to be? Did you become it?
>
> How did your goals and dreams turn out? Were they altered as life took its inevitable twists in the road?
>
> When you think of the Great Moments in your life, are they the moments you thought they would be?
>
> Where did you rise, and where did you fall?
>
> What, if any, are your regrets looking back? Is there a way to fix them? Have you fixed them? Do you need to, or is it best to pay it forward elsewhere?

These are some of the questions I've been pondering lately. Some were easy to answer, some not so much. They have given me endless things to reflect on and improve upon. Maybe you will think on them for a while. Then ask yourself, what is left on your list?

Life is full of twists and turns. That is a beautiful thing. All we can hope for at the end of our days is a life well lived. There are always ups and downs, and if there weren't, what a meager existence it would be. It is the delicate tapestry of joy and suffering that gives our lives their richness.

A young man I worked with briefly shared one day that when he was a kid his father told him, "It's not what happens to you, it's how you deal with it". What a gem of insight! Best thing that came out of that whole gig! Thanks Anthony!

How will you deal with it? "It" in this case being this remainder of your life. What is left on your list?

These are the magical days when we can determine our future, our legacy, and how we want to be remembered in this world. If we are lucky, we have become wise. Are you using your special talents and abilities to serve the greater good? Each of us has the power to make this world a better place. Every one of us has a different role to fill. What were you put here to do? Not your career necessarily, but your will?

And beyond duty, consider your own desires. What goals do you still want to pursue? What do you want to be doing now? Are there unrealized dreams?

How do you want to feel? Is there unreleased trauma holding you back from knowing true happiness? Are there things you need to make right? Are there coping mechanisms you want to shed before you shed this mortal coil?

What is left on your list?

If there has been struggle with your self image, now is the time to get through the things that have been holding you back from being comfortable in your own skin. We are all beautiful and all flawed.

It's time to take responsibility for who we are, and the decisions we made for whatever reason. Forgive yourself, be kinder to yourself, and let's build a better tomorrow. Most of us probably have some trauma to release or "shadow work" to push through. If not now, when? Why take those chains to your grave?

Several years ago, I realized I had developed some odd thinking patterns and coping mechanisms that no longer served me. I worked to be a better friend to myself and quell my angry inner critics. A happy side effect from that was I found having personal boundaries much easier. It's freeing to finally see and understand my flawed thinking about myself and how it affected my judgment. I could be disappointed it took me to this age, but I say better late than never, I am thankful to have let it go! But that's a whole other story.

There are so many millions of ways to make the world better and find joy, in this part of our life as much as any other. Maybe more. Even if we just come to a better understanding of ourselves, we help make the world better. So, what's left on YOUR list?

FORGETTiNG OUR POWER... NO MORE!

We are intuitives, and life givers. We are the most powerful of all creatures but the subjugation of our species based on sex has rendered us shallow bowls, handing our power away for millennia. Stop this! Tell your children and grandchildren.

Such sad foolishness, worrying about our weight, or what others think, fed on media propaganda to keep us downtrodden and angry at our fellow women. From Eve to Pandora to Cleopatra, we are change makers, and we have brought out the greatness in men since time immemorial. In polytheistic societies, the ancient Greeks, the Norse, Hindu, and more, from Ireland to the bottom of South America, such faiths worship female deities as much as or even more than male gods.

You can say there is not precedence in our modern era, no role models to look to, I say bullshit. One of my idols, a female photographer began taking photos as a grandmother in the late 19th century, and much like Vincent Van Gogh, Julia Margaret Cameron's work was derided and ridiculed in her day. Today it is appreciated for the master art it is. She created still theater using everyone she could get to pose - family, neighbors, servants.

Women have defied society and the odds forever, it's just no one likes to talk about their accomplishments or accept how big some of them were. Scientists like Marie Curie, Margaret Mead and Rachel Carson. Authors like Agatha Christie, Ursula LeGuin, Margaret Atwood, and Ayn Rand. Photographers like Julia Margaret Cameron, Dorothea Lange, Mary Ellen Mark; journalists such as Naomi Klein and Amy Goodman; society women like Bertha Palmer or Jane Addams. Women who rose like Maya Angelou. Women who changed the world against all odds like Helen Keller. There are women who spoke out strong like Buffy St Marie, Wendy O Williams, and Nina Simone. Women who made a mark in different ways, like Julia Child, Hedy Lamar, or Lucille Ball. They remain minimized, women's ever humble assists taken for granted.

Let's admit there is a lot of needless suffering in the world. We are allowing for animals to go extinct, for children to go hungry, for bombs to be dropped on people all over the world. You ever see those images of birds or marine life where their stomachs are full of colorful plastic? Hate to say, our insides look the same. We've been fed plastic for years, decades, in addition to GMOs, pesticides, and whatever is coming off those darn Teflon pans.

If all living things are linked, if all humans share a collective unconscious, then the only way to stop our epidemics of trauma damage and depression, the plagues of diabetes and chronic pain, is to work toward ending the suffering of all beings. For those of us who eat meat, most of the livestock today live an entire life of suffering. How is that nourishing us?

This change to a disposable world happened in my lifetime, and I believe we can fix it.

We are women, microcosms of the Earth itself. We heal, we create, we nurture. It's time to tap into our calling, to heal ourselves, to love each other, and to change the world. Seems like a big ask. But is it? There are 168 hours in a week, can you spare a few to help another? Can you spare one or two to learn something new? Can you find a few to get involved in guiding government? When we remember our power, our strength, and our ability to unite, we can achieve anything.

Have I mentioned The Donner Party? Do you know about them? A group of pioneers took a bad route west and got stuck in a 100 year snow storm. They turned to cannibalism before the summer thaw came, is how history speaks of them, however there is another part to that story. Most of the survivors were actually the women, not because they became crazed hatchet killers. That was the men. The women pooled together little things they had, from a few tablespoons of lard to a leather shoe sole, they made soups and stews and tried to avoid the mania. The women survived because they came together and shared their resources. Many of the men died in fights and conflicts with one another and not actually from starvation. Yet, in that same moment of desperation, the women came back to their power, their will. Do you think they all agreed on politics or interpretations of the Bible? Doubtful. At some point natural law won out over man's laws.

To hell with man's laws, those have given us suffering and subjugation. So many worship one who hung on a cross, but how many women have burned at the stake in anonymity? No more! Arise! Embrace your true nature.

WHERE CAN WE STAND? WiLL YOU HOLD MY HAND?

We have so much untapped power and potential together. But there is a lot of anger and ignorance and marketing that we need to get past. We women have had a hard time getting along. The entire idea of frenemies is really weird. We have been pitted against one another for decades. We are taught so often to measure ourselves us against each other, against models and celebrity exaggerations of women.

Did you know it took women until 1920 to officially be able to vote? A campaign was begun in 1848, and took until 1920. Freed black men earned the right to vote and run for office in 1870 in our nation's 15th amendment. Women's voting rights came as our 19th amendment and took another 50 years. Do you know why that is? In researching for an article I wrote back in 2004 about the long fight for a woman's right to vote. I learned the sad delay of nearly a century came down to one thing: Bitches couldn't get along.

There was one side of the suffragists led by Susan B. Anthony that demanded temperance be part of the amendment, something akin to prohibition. It was on the stance that drunkenness led to domestic violence. The other side of the suffragist movement was working class women, many whom worked in bars and taverns, they did not want to lose that livelihood, nor the culture, and they certainly didn't want it tied to their vote. They wanted the vote. One had nothing to do with the other.

Ironically, the amendment that started Prohibition came three years before women had the right to vote. The amendment that created income tax also came before women had the vote.

Enter Edward Bernays, the man who invented modern marketing as the practice of preying on our human weaknesses and desires. He sidled up to the suffragists and told them if they wanted to be equal to men, they ought to start smoking on the protest lines! He did this to create a "new market" for Philip Morris Tobacco Company. He was also Sigmund Freud's nephew. I talk a lot about marketing in these pages, but marketing is a big part of the problem. Marketing. Fashion. Propaganda. In so many we ways we barely recognize it. It is poison.

They sow this divide between us, but most of us are in the same struggle. The struggle of survival when housing prices have tripled, but pay rates have stagnated and even gone down over the last 30 years. We are at the end of the line with this economic system. The super rich are planning their bunkers and rockets into space. We are on our own if anything goes down. Rather than fighting, what if we came together? We do not need the government to save the rain forest, we just need enough people to stand firm. Is that you?

WHAT COULD WE DO TOGETHER?

We have a great deal of power as individuals. These may in fact be our most powerful years. We are the matriarchs! Let us each step into that role with energy and compassion. We have five generations behind us we need to assist.

Together we are more than a voting block, we are powerful in so many bigger ways. It doesn't matter if you wear a red hat or a blue hat, a cowboy hat or a tiara, we all want the same basic things. We want a good life for ourselves and those we love. We want our children and grandchildren to enjoy fresh air and clean water, we want them to have the best education they can, and not be left with debt they will never pay off. We want to see a doctor when we need to, and if a loved one experiences a major illness we want them to have the care they need without a mountain of debt that renders them homeless six months later. We all deserve the unencumbered pursuit of happiness.

Basically, these things we agree on are forever. The media and our elected officials always have a finger to point, but never any solutions. All of our politicians are millionaires. They are not statesmen, they are looking out for numero uno, themselves and their wallets. They have sold out our drinking water to corporations, they have allowed hundreds of mountains to be blasted away for coal. They are constant warmongers, creating conflicts with any nation who doesn't want our western ways. Meanwhile, we have the largest prison population the world. Just recently laws were passed in the USA to allow children under age 16 to work overnight in slaughterhouses and meat packing factories.

When every problem facing us as a people, as a society, and civilization is "systemic", then logic would say we need to build a new system! I will say that again and again. Seems pretty simple.

Let's start with our elections, let's stop corporate funding and donations, period. No more political commercials. The politicians today are not the eloquent learned men of the past, they are rich guys who were born rich, and that privilege has allowed them to remain ignorant and isolated. They are power hungry. I'm not meaning to sound political, but you might have noticed, things are a mess.

Fighting for freedom, warring for peace, ha! What a crock of total bullshit. I saw some bathroom graffiti once that said "War for peace is like fucking for virginity". Sorry if that is crude, it was bathroom graffiti, I warned you. Oh cover thy delicate eyes if that offended ye! It might be crass, it's also truth.

What is it you hate about your neighbor? Is it something they actually did, or something you are perceiving about them? The differences in our experiences and our lives are great and valuable. If we were all the same, we would not have made it this far. Our diversity, the utopian concept of the melting pot, is what makes America so special. There is so much we can learn from one another, so much we can achieve together. But when we separate ourselves by our differences, we all lose.

Rather than build walls around ourselves of urban or rural, sophisticated or simple, by color or ethnicity, by age and sex, by our level of masculinity and femininity, our religion or political bent, we need to take our neighbor's hands and bridge those gaps, share knowledge and wisdom with one another.

Years back, I found myself sharing pizza with a couple in Kentucky. The couple was delightful. Tommy was a Christian preacher and life coach, and Tammy, a church organist and photographer. I was married then, and my husband and I were the exact opposite of what they were, yet we were having great conversations over dinner. One of us commented how it was such a great time with them, even though we were seemingly polar opposites in regard to faith or ideology. Tommy said "The reason we can talk openly is because we are comfortable with our beliefs and our faith. Nothing you can say is going to change my views on Jesus, and it is the same for you". He said problems arise when people aren't strong in their own beliefs, then they are afraid of someone with an opposite belief because of their own lack of faith. That made a lot of sense.

Let's take abortion for example. A hot button subject. I am 100% pro-choice, and I can make my case to anyone. Why? Because I have looked at this from every side. First and foremost, no one, not one person wants to have an abortion. When the situation arises it is after much internal debate and personal agony. However, sometimes it is the best thing, for whatever reason. I am not going to put circumstance on it, just sometimes a woman cannot carry a child, and she has to make this terribly hard decision.

Outlawing abortion will not stop abortion. It will make it less safe and harder to get, which will cause desperate women to take desperate measures that could cost them their lives and/or their fertility. I can understand why people feel so loathsome about abortion, it is terrible. But it needs to be a legally available terrible to keep women safe, and it needs to be a last resort. There needs to be a better understanding of our bodies, our fertility, birth control, and sex. Nobody on either side of this topic wants people harmed. That much we can agree on.

Parents don't want their small children to be forced to learn about sex as school curriculum, and that makes sense too. We don't want to sexualize our children too early, but maybe around 12 or 13 there needs to be some program of study that teaches all boys and girls about their bodies, about safe sex, about the difference between desire and readiness for sex, about a girl's cycle. Some will disagree with me, but I believe a vast majority of us wish we knew more about our bodies growing up, and especially about our physical and emotional needs.

How many young women got pregnant before abortion was legal and were sent away, forced to give these babies up for adoption? Many. While maybe not one of these young women wished for an abortion, I bet all of them wished they had better understood the weight of having sex. I bet they wished they knew more about safe sex, and about being ready - not just physically but also emotionally, and about being able to say no.

Which brings us to society's teaching of girls to be agreeable and acquiesce, while at the same time celebrating a lack of responsibility for one's actions with "boys will be boys". While boys will be boys, part of that should not be being a rapist. Perhaps we simply need to stop mutilating the genitals of baby boys with circumcision, maybe that would stop the rage inside them that feeds the war machine, creates rapists, and violent domestic partners?

So ladies, we have our work cut out for us here. Could we stop listening to the talking heads on the news? Could we stop supporting politicians who can barely put a sentence together but have more money than our family line combined, more than our entire neighborhood put together, and some entire nations? How did they get there? Why did we prop them up?

I for one will never vote for the "lesser of two evils" again. I want to vote for a human being who wants to make life better for everyone, not just their donors. I'll gladly throw it up to a lottery! Give me Ralph the electrician or Sally the grocery clerk as governor, senator, president, over any long generations of wicked money!

If we stood united and strong, we could move mountains to create a better world. I have a hundred ideas to make the world better, you probably do too, so does your neighbor, and even your "rival", so let's put down the foolish divides and learn from our sisters, and teach our sisters. I bet we agree on enough of the important stuff to make a difference toward what could be a really beautiful world.

When we remember our power, we will rise. We can fix this. Our mother the Earth calls. The goddesses who have reigned and been worshiped beg you to remember your power. Remember your might. Unite & fight!

AGING IS A CRIME, AND OTHER MYTHICAL BS

Aging is a crime in America, it seems. Women are in a weird lose/lose game of losing as far as society goes when it comes to aging. Modern western society has told us aging is not allowed for women. While we admire the "distinguished man", the aged woman is little more than the butt of jokes.

Hollywood starlets must stay young or they betray the world by growing old, and if they try desperately to hold onto youth by surgical or other invasive means, we scoff at them. Men and women alike are guilty of this. I recall as a youth how much disdain the actress Elizabeth Taylor was treated with for getting old when in the late 1980s she took a brief role on the soap opera 'General Hospital'. We see it with Madonna now and her bloated cheeks of plastic filler.

As a woman, if you grow old gracefully, you are shamed for it. If one uses artificial means to appear potentially younger, society mocks her for that. If she still dresses in a youthful way she is foolish. If she has become matronly she has shamed herself. Ironically, being "old" here as a woman is a crime, but in other cultures elder women are regarded as most high, not unlike our friend the orca. There are ceremonial garments only elder women can wear in far eastern, middle eastern, Native American and other cultures, and there are certain roles reserved for them, powerful roles.

I noticed one day my social media feed was full of wrinkle cream ads with women too young to have any wrinkles. It made me wonder how long I had been buying wrinkle cream myself? Since 30 maybe, 32? How absurd. (Further, there's a difference between wrinkles and lines. Lines are who you are, whereas wrinkles are from dehydration and lack of moisture. Yeah, some creams are better than others, but price has little to do with it. Make your own if you can, and read the labels if you buy it. A lot of face creams and cosmetics are toxic.)

Then I had the freeing realization that I, the women in the wrinkle cream ads, Madonna, Liz Taylor, and all the rest of us are victims of marketing. Marketing told me I needed wrinkle cream when I was barely more than a child. Women trying to hold onto their youth rather than embracing their now are all victims of marketing and the tools of marketing too! Why was anyone looking to advertising for answers?

Now I see it for what it is. It's what it always was, lies told to us to make us insecure and eagerly buying into a lifetime of products that prey on the fears in us that they created. Of course we have always adorned ourselves in various ways throughout time. That is adornment for empowerment. This is modification due to weakness and insecurity. Today's shallowness is likely a symbol of collapse in itself. If we are all staring in the mirror, we are not fulfilling ourselves. There is a difference between vanity and taking a long hard look at oneself. That is vital. A world of perfect smiling advert models is universal fear mongering to keep people always scrambling to find their place, measuring themselves against, and trying to take from others.

We are all taught to be insecure by marketing. If we feel good about ourselves, we are not good consumers, but if we are feeling bad about our looks, our weight, our age, what the neighbors have, what life looks like on TV, we are miserable. Ever consider how much money big pharma is raking in on our fears, sorrows, and insecurities alone? Think about it. Many millions of people take prescriptions every single day, just to be able to get through their dreary day, but why are our days dreary?

Is it because we have done everything we were told to do to measure up to society and it still isn't enough? Or because we hate our jobs and careers? Or we married the wrong person or we grew apart but stay together? How many people are miserable in their marriage because that's what they were shown on TV? Men reach a certain age and they thirst for a sports car and a new young thing, to make them feel alive. But is that true? Or is that what has been beaten into their head since they were 18, that at 50 they will be miserable with their life? I bet the sports car dealers, and the plastic surgeons, and the weight loss gurus are all very happy to have you believe these fallacies. Modern humans are making them rich with all the needs they have to fill the holes in their souls and their lives because marketing told them the holes were there.

So you know what I say about it all? Fuck that! Fuck society! I am not interested in being part of any society that doesn't value all people, that doesn't value nature, that worships money as god. Any group who doesn't value the wisdom of the elder is essentially degrading and DE-evolving. We have become a weak, ignorant, and stupid society. Divided by perceived differences. We believe so many stupid things presented to us as fact, and as science even! We believe the news. We fall right in line to hate those with differing views, but is that true or did marketing - including the media, create those views and divides? It's gross.

We are told in today's world that old people have no value, but that couldn't be further from the truth! All these young people today, trying to homestead, canning and living off the land, rediscovering old knowledge, or trying to and failing. Meanwhile the people with the knowledge they seek are withering alone in nursing homes. That is truly the crime.

BEiNG A WOMAN iS A MiSDEMEANOR

Honestly, if I consider it deeply, being a woman at all in modern society is criminal, *persona non grata*. In my childhood, I recall news reports of people in China throwing infant daughters out the window or dumping them in the trash because it was more honorable to have sons. There was a big campaign afoot for a while to adopt these Chinese baby girls to American families because of it. But looking back, who knows if that was true or propaganda. Maybe these baby girls were grabbed from the clutches of loving parents? It's hard to say, but that's how the USA media portrayed it at the time, and why? Was it to further let women here know they don't matter anywhere?

In our world today, things have never been more backwards. Women in porn, strippers, or in the sex trade are expected to be such exaggerations of women that no regular woman can live up to, not even the women portraying these exaggerations. I've heard men speak so derogatorily of women who get breast implants, yet at the same time they say they want a woman with big boobs. It's disturbed thinking and yet it is prevailing culture. The whole concept of these anime characters and the filters on social media are just more caricaturization of women, more never measuring up. How many buff dude filters are there versus filters to make women look flawless and "perfect"? I get that dress-up and costumes are fun, but it's not real life and it should not be an expectation that it is.

Then we get to all the modifications done en masse today as cosmetic surgery, many of them bound to go wrong, and all implants needing replacement every decade or so. There is the general lack of treatment, and direct mis-treatment of women under the guise of practicing medicine. Research on women's health is minuscule. Things like heart stents are not tested on women. Women's medical care is generally dismissive and historically lacking. Today, doctors just lop off women's breasts for breast cancer, potential breast cancer, and now for the tragic "top surgery" trend. Did top surgery become the new breast implant to pay off those tremendous student loans doctors have? Women are constantly encouraged to disfigure themselves in the name of beauty, of so-called health, in the name of potential risk, and even as a cure to sexuality, asexuality, gender fluidity, and/or sexual trauma. Look at the baby powder lawsuits of recent years: we were urged by marketing to cover up "embarrassing odor" with baby powder on our privates, but it sadly turns out it gave women cancer, cysts, and infertility.

Women today still do most of the housework and other domestic duties no matter how large the family, even as breadwinner or co-breadwinner. In our careers we have had to run faster, be smarter, and do more than every man in our position. We still live in a world of earning seventy cents to every dollar men earn in our same positions. We are gaslit and dismissed of any achievement earned individually or collectively. Look at all the women in science, art, and other fields who have changed or are changing the world yet we never hear about them. Why didn't I learn about Margaret Mead in elementary school? Why aren't women like Vandana Shiva, Amy Goodman, and Phylis Yes household names like their male counterparts are? There's no lack of examples to prove my case, it's criminal. It's a human tragedy that western women have been trained to be so insecure.

BAD HiSTORiCAL PRECEDENCE

Years back, I read an article in a magazine that purported in Ancient Egypt, widows often jumped or were pushed into the fire burning their deceased husband. Self-immolation. It doesn't seem like much has changed. Certainly elderly single men are lonely, but there is something so pathetic in modern depictions of old women.

All those 1970s horror movies sure did not help, with the old spinster witches and the lurking evil often held in the old widow's house, or villainous old ladies like in 'Arsenic and Old Lace'. Or the angry narrow-minded nosy neighbor, or the forgotten woman all alone waiting for the phone to ring.

In India, if a woman is widowed she is stripped of her status and belongings and tossed into the street. Can you imagine throwing your dear old mum into the street because she dared to outlive your father? There are cities full of these widows, they gather in hovels and churches and "wait to die". How macabre! Think about that, it's happening today in a nation turning out many of our highly skilled engineers and doctors. How much compassion can we expect from people with that mindset? I'm not slighting India, America acts similar.

A hundred years ago, most homes in America were intergenerational. There might be aunts, uncles, cousins, grandparents, and great-grandparents all under one roof. Other cultures still practice this, but not us fancy pants westerners. Today we have assisted living facilities. Did you know most are funded and run by investment companies? Their focus is on profits, and very little on actual care and community for our honored citizens.

Rolling into my mid 50s, I don't feel at all ready for the 55+ community. How about you? And even if you are sitting in one, or in an assisted living center, or even in a widow city in India, this doesn't have to be the dismal end. There is no reason the end of our days must include the end of joy and happiness for months, years, maybe decades before we die. A great woman I knew, Miriam Atkins once said, "you don't have to be what they said you were." That statement holds true for this part of our life. We don't have to be the widow forever in black, or the throwaway. We can make these days count as much as, and maybe more than any of those before it!

THE STRANGER IN THE MiRROR

At some point, this old just isn't gonna wash off.

Many of us fret about our changing faces. So much so that millions, actually billions, is spent annually on surgeries, creams, and a myriad of treatments to slow aging or appear younger. Yet we have always changed. We've grown from childhood and changed and morphed so many times, why so much fear about this? Imagine, we were once tiny babies! Why stress on the changing face? Is it because we were told old people were faded and out of touch, or old is ugly? As with most prejudice, the person purporting it has the problem, not the people they dislike. Some people say babies are ugly, imagine. Blanket criticism typically says much more about the complainer than their target. If someone has issue with the lines on my face, it's their issue and I feel bad for them.

Don't be ashamed of the face you are seeing now in the mirror and the reflection that is to come. Think of how beautiful autumn leaves are, and yet they are death to the leaf. So it goes, my friend. This is the ride we are on, 'The Great Is All' that is this life. It's actually a really short ride. We are sharing this moment, each of us and all those around us are on our own path and in different stages of life, heading to our own future. It's all beautiful. It's all precious. Do not be shamed by the changing face in the mirror. You are still you.

So much of this shame we have in aging, especially as women, is purely from marketing. Simple commodification creating the demand for "beauty" products that we do not need. Corporations have been preying on us for decades, creating things to be insecure about so they could sell us products, many of them poison. Did you know sunscreen is killing the coral reefs? Oxybenzone. If it's highly toxic to marine life, what is it doing to our skin? How is that allowed?

In Victorian times, women powdered their faces with arsenic. It's why society ladies were always fainting and often dying in childbirth. Do you think anything has changed?

For corporations, it is simply creating a market by creating feelings of insecurity within us. You see all those products available to help us with our cellulite, our loose skin, our anything and our everything, but it's just preying on our psyches to get the money from our wallets. None of these measures are valid at all!!

A lot of that is simple sexist oppression, and the worst part? It exists because we allow it to exist. We perpetuate it.

What is beauty? It is truly in the eye of the beholder. One man's queen is another man's throwaway. One woman's dud is another woman's stud. So much of this sham of insecurity has been manufactured and really holds no place in reality if we consider it seriously. Love and acceptance will never come via wrinkle cream. People are attracted to all different people. Unless we are totally vain and shallow, we care about people because they add value to our lives. They bring us joy and friendship, intimacy and comfort. Attraction in the sexual sense is based on a complex myriad of things, including our electromagnetic waves and our pheromones. And then of course our interests, passions, and personality.

No life of true substance is measured in the mirror. Supermodels? Sure you got me there. But even they have to be more than their face and body to have a truly happy life. I can say with all certainty there are supermodels, actresses and actors, great celebrities of every variety who feel bad about themselves. They are empty inside because they fed into society. We all do it. But, we can't live there. Wasting time on what is in the mirror is foolishness.

Consider this: if you look at most of the sex symbols of modern times, those we can see in actual photos and video, they are not classical, stone chiseled beauties, but they emanate a sexiness, a confidence, and beauty from within. It's their real or perceived sense of self that makes them irresistibly attractive.

When we consider the meaningful people, places and events of our lives, the good times had very little to do with how ripped our abs were. Even in my youth, my weight had very little to do with my actual happiness. I've had many of the greatest moments of my life being perhaps pleasantly plump, or with a bad haircut, or having the wrong shoes on.

If I am enjoying life, my body image is usually pretty good no matter if I have a pimple, or an extra 20 pounds. If I am miserable, it doesn't matter how thin I am or how perfect my makeup is, nothing is good enough. If you are feeling good about your life and yourself it shows, and things will tend more to go your way. Good things happen. If we stomp around in anger, self-pity, or regret, more negative circumstances present themselves. That is math and science more than counting our age.

The face in the mirror looks beautiful if we are smiling.

When we are feeling down, we see every flaw we perceive we have, real or imagined. That is all us, our reflection and our inner being. For me, if I am having a good time then I am not worrying about my appearance. If I'm uncomfortable in a situation or inside myself, I am aware of the pinch in my shoe or my too tight sweater. In which scenario am I more attractive? If I relax and am having fun, I exude beauty. Same as you, same as anyone. It would seem then, the reflection in the mirror is more about how we feel inside, so maybe instead of fretting about lines and wrinkles we just do more stuff that brings us joy and happiness.

I'm not trying to candy coat this process. Sure, some days doubt creeps in, and fear of getting older. It isn't easy. It's hard to think about this one way ride. I realize now the people who didn't get here maybe got out easy. I used to think living was easier than dying. Both are hard. It's hard to look in the mirror and not recognize the face I saw for so long, but then I look into my eyes and I smile at myself in the mirror and I see that I am still there. I am still vital and alive. I am still full of wonder for each day, and I am thankful every dusk and dawn for my existence.

Maybe this special time of not seeing ourselves in the mirror is a gift to us? We no longer need to try to live up to society's false standards. We are free!!! Now we can move on to the important work of the day. This world needs us. It needs us strong and resolute.

The world needs us to show the way. We have seen it all. We have observed, we have protected and built, we have nurtured and sought. We can use our varied skills and we can make a mark on this world. We can leave this place better than we found it.

We can help our sisters, daughters, and grandchildren. We can help all of us, we can build up each other and our communities. We can share substance over salve, purpose instead of panic over "lost looks". We are beautiful by our deeds, our thoughts, and our character. We are lovely in the way we lead. Step up, and the person in the mirror will remain beautiful forever.

GEODES AND AGING

Around my house I have a few small geodes. One is white with clear crystals inside it. One is a deep purple inside - it looks like a half eaten blueberry hand pie - and the third is a strange pale blue with a tiny shimmery center. I could marvel at them for hours. They are magical!

When I was a child, our next door neighbors once brought my parents a half geode and a whole un-cracked geode as souvenirs from a family vacation. It was a thank you gift for feeding and caring for their dog while they were gone. The geodes were around the size of softballs and I was fascinated such a thing could exist. The half geode was clear crystal inside, all perfect geometric squares glistening and sparkling in the sunlight. My parents never cracked the full geode open, so who knows what marvels lay inside of it? I remember how it was perfectly round with bumps, like a tiny moon, and it was so heavy. I was certain they were some kind of otherworldly receiver. I still believe that about them. We are just too ignorant in our current incarnation to see their power and energy. We've lost so much knowledge over time.

Anyway, one day as I marveled at the deep purple crystal inside the "blueberry pie" half geode, I realized I never really looked at the outside of it, only at it incredible glittering inside. For as much as I pick up rocks on my walks, I never studied the outside of my geodes so I could maybe find some.

I turned it around and was taken aback by it's homely appearance. A gray crusty shell of bumps and ridges, it seemed potentially unpleasant to behold. I picked up the blue one, and then the largest, the clear crystalline one, and I turned them all on their back side. I was stunned. Had I seen any of these whole lying in the earth I would never have guessed at the beauty held inside!

I decided I needed to turn all the geodes around for a while, to learn to love the outsides of them. I didn't know why but it seemed important. Slowly I began to understand. I had always just stared into the remarkable insides of these incredible little gifts from the earth, I told myself I needed to realize the beauty of their outsides. It wasn't easy. While stunning in some ways, I would probably have ignored any one of them on a rocky shoreline or trail. I'd think it was a sand formation, or maybe even a creature. This made me look deeper into the outer crusts and marvel at the exquisite bumps and lumps.

After a few months of looking at the backs of my three little geodes, I realized what a great analogy geodes offer for aging. These are perhaps the geode years, when the content of our character, or what is on the inside is where the real beauty is, and was all along. As we get older, our shell is potentially dulled or masked, so we need to open ourselves and share our amazing inside beauty! Inside we are still the dazzling crystalline treasure we always were, if not more so.

In fact, I am looking at these geodes again as I write this, hoping they will shine their power and energy upon me and this project. While this manifesto is being written for a very specific group, I want it to be so that any person who might pick it up and read it would come away with an improved spirit and better understanding.

The inside of my geode is here currently. I am putting it down, presented on these pages. The inside of my geode is doing my best in all of my endeavors. It is treating everyone I encounter with kindness and understanding, a friendly hello on the street. The dazzle of the geode has always been inside of us. This is the time to truly let that inside shine.

MY IRRATIONAL FEAR OF
THE INDEPENDENT WOMEN OF ASTORIA

In 2008, through happenstance, I landed at the mouth of the Columbia River, into the rural Oregon/Washington coastal community. It wasn't some dream I had to live there. I hadn't known the place existed until a week or two before that, but something about it charmed me. It felt like home the moment I arrived. Our plan was to stay two weeks, then a month. We ended up living there for a decade.

It was an old fishing community, with summer visitors coming in the warm months. It was moving toward a full visitor and retiree community. On the Washington side was the Long Beach Peninsula, a 26-mile long sand spit. Back in 2008, it still had the feel of a down and out old boardwalk town and offered guaranteed, low paying, summer work which was the reason we had traveled there. The entire experience was a great growing experience for me, in so many ways. I started my own little business and my lousy, low paying jobs got better and better. I felt like I was really taking charge of my life. Or at least my "come what may" attitude about the direction of my life was actually paying off.

Anyway, one of the odd things about the place, especially on the Oregon side in Astoria, was the number of older single women. Aside all these fishing families, Scandinavians, retired couples, drifters old and new, rugged individuals, and former inmates looking to get on a fishing boat at the end of the world because nothing else was working, was this very distinct population of older women who were uncoupled, apparently by choice, and I have to admit they terrified me. They were not scary in any way. On the contrary, they were amazing, lovely ladies, and I am thankful to have become fairly well acquainted with a couple of them over the years.

I don't mean they lived together like the widow cities of India. They all lived in their own places all over the area, some in town, some further out on land. They weren't a group like the Red Hat Society ladies. I am certain they in no way saw themselves as a group of any kind as I am linking them here. There wasn't a club, most probably didn't even know each other. It was just my own observation that there were a large number of independently living older women, lets say 50 and up, who seemed to be choosing to be on their own.

Initially, in my ignorance as a married person, I thought how lonely that must be for them. Surely they wanted a significant other? Over time I got to know a few of them. Each was completely remarkable. None of them appeared to be looking or longing for a partner.

Visiting over a joint and coffee one day, Jane said she was upset about some hefty yard work she needed to do. "You don't understand, things are a lot easier with two people. There's only so much I can do alone." She said, but it wasn't like she had any interest in finding a guy to help her. I mean sure, she hired a landscaper, but she wasn't wishing for a partner to assist. She was self-made. Jane had done plenty on her own. She owned her house, she said she bought it in the 1980s from doing hair. She's been a puppet maker and a theater designer, she's a respected painter, an artist in so many ways! She had many male friends, and I'm sure plenty of suitors, but she didn't seem at all interested in having a partner in any permanent way.

Another, Carol who called herself a "New York Jew", was living outside of town on a bucolic road with rolling hills and old time farmhouses. She had a degree in folk dancing, and last I heard she was still hosting a weekly radio show on the community station. She confided that she had come to the community because of a man, but the relationship didn't work out. She stayed because she loved the area. She contributes so much to the community in every way, for probably 30 years now, and supports the arts aggressively. She always supported our projects. She attended our events and was deeply encouraging.

I met Wenda because she was giving away a welder and wanted it to go another artist. My former husband was the lucky recipient, and when we went to pick it up we learned what an amazing folk artist she is. We instantly became friends and we would look forward to visiting with her if we saw her volunteering at the Liberty Theater or if she had an arts show going.

All of them are amazing women, creative, talented and independent. Today, I can smile about how intimidated I was by their independence. Such strong individuals, each living life on their own terms. Self-made and sometimes outspoken. Not cowering away, but out in the community, being change makers, building the community they wanted to see.

Back then, I found myself concerned for their loneliness. I'm sure they were sometimes lonely, but so was I, and I was married! Surely, we all have periods of loneliness, no matter how alone or surrounded we are.

I remember wondering how they had the strength and the ability to go it alone. I found it impressive, but also terrifying. I admired them. I still admire them. I felt they were everything I could never be. How were they doing it on their own? And, even more, how could they choose that?

Just typing that question gives me pause today. My own foolishness to think that of course, everyone is looking for a significant other. Perhaps the reason they shine so bright is because they had no one blocking their light. And, who knows what kinds of great relationships they had going. You can have love and not have "a partner". In other writings about them I've speculated that the sea beckoned to them as its brides, and the roaring masculine energy of the mouth of the Columbia filled them up. Wow.

It is funny how my perception of them has changed. My perception, not them. Ah, but I have learned so much these last few years, especially about what a successful relationship is. It starts with a successful relationship with one's self. I don't know if I can ever be as self-made and self-assured as the independent ladies of Astoria, but I can try.

TAKiNG CARE OF VESSELS, OR ONLY FLOSS THE ONES YOU WANT TO KEEP

In some weird way, I feel lucky that my marriage fell apart just over a year before the pandemic began in March 2020. As lucky as one can be when a 20-some year relationship crashes and burns in devastating heartbreak. I was already recuperating from that when we all hunkered down for what we were told would be "a two-week lockdown" to "flatten the curve". Remember that? Ha. I was able to have a lot more levity with that whole Surrealist nightmare because I'd already spent a year living in my own version of that landscape, and I had already made a number of healthy changes in my life.

In my teens I announced, "Adversity builds character", and over the years I have built a lot of character. Funny, I had so many pronouncements as a kid. I wish I'd had more confidence, or I wish I had mentors that were themselves not so beaten down. I could not see the wisdom of my words. There was an oppressiveness where I grew up. A kind of "no one gets out alive" mentality. People will cling to ignorance or suffering if it is what they know, if it is familiar. Outside the walls is unknown and unknown is scary.

It has taken me a long time to really believe I deserve better. I spent too much time feeling unlovable because I was less than perfect. But, who is perfect? Nobody. It's been challenging to let go of lack, my feeling that I lack the power to make a difference, or control my own life, or I don't deserve to have my voice heard in the world. But I've given up on being beaten down. What makes anyone else better than me? Nothing. We can all be noble or ignoble. I live by my deeds and how I express my values into the world. I have succeeded and failed at living up to my values, but I always strive to do what is right.

How much of ill health is born from that alone -- letting ourselves down, or acting in a wrong manner? How much from going against the gut when you know you are right, or doing something against what you know is right? It wears on our health and well-being probably more than any germ. How much Irritable Bowel Syndrome is trauma, intuition denied, or triggers from repressed events?

Part of the cultivation of my own self-worth and value was taking better care of myself. Not because I wanted to look good or date, but because I felt like I was going to die of a broken heart. My grandmother had, and so had my uncle. My chest was killing me in those early weeks after my husband just walked out of my life one night. It felt like my heart was going to explode, I had fitful sleep and terrible dreams, and so much grief I was suffering.

I began doing yoga to try to ease the pain and at least say I tried. Ironically, five years down the road, I have held onto this practice. And while I have veered off for a few weeks here or there, I always come back to it. Learning and relearning the practice. It is truly now part of my life and has fulfilled me in so many ways.

"Only floss the ones you want to keep." My sister told me her dentist said that to her. I found this tragically hilarious. I don't know if flossing is really the be all end all of tooth health, but I can appreciate it's part of it. Bad teeth will shorten our lives. I recently met a couple of young men who are very bright and personable, attractive, hardworking, but their teeth are nearly rotted away. It breaks my heart. How did we fail them so miserably? Where were we as parents, teachers, and other role models that we forgot to teach these two young men the importance of caring for their teeth? In this world, the alleged richest nation in the world, no one should be unable to seek dental care.

If I was a dentist, I would feel duty bound to help people in this situation. Not as some kick back, not using them as unwitting test subjects for some villainous thing. That should not enter into the minds of people. Why does it?

If everyone is suffering and struggling, are we really the richest? It's like saying Walmart prices are low. Yes, their prices are low in the store, but that "value" costs us when all of their employees are still qualifying for government survival benefits. The sweatpants may have a $9.88 price tag, but we all paid perhaps $500 this year out of our paychecks for their employees to have food stamps and medical care at government expense, while the store's owners rake in millions in profit by not providing living wages and benefits.

I remember working in an office years back and one of my office mates, a really lovely, soft spoken man in his late forties, ate fast food every single day for lunch. I asked him why? "I like it!" was his response. He wasn't concerned about his health being affected by whatever bad stuff I felt was in the food. This same man had several bouts of brain cancer, resulting in numerous life threatening surgeries, and yet he had fast food everyday. I'm always amazed when people have an unwavering belief that multinational corporations care about their customers. There was a time when maybe that was the case, when food was actually food. But not today, now it's all about "Bottom Line Thinking".

Don't get me started on "Bottom Line Thinking".

Maybe this is the perfect place to talk about bottom line thinking. It is the plague of modern man. It is the reason diabetes is epidemic, and 700 square foot houses are $500,000. Any person who starts a sentence with "The bottom line is..." is your enemy. There was a time when beauty was thought of in every single thing created by man. Now we think, what is the cheapest it can be done? How can I cut corners? How can I get mine... at the expense of others, nature, the planet, my integrity? Look at old houses and chairs and watches. The detail and craftsmanship was immaculate. Even budget goods were in good working order and as beautiful as they could possibly be.

My favorite architect, Louis Sullivan, the man who created the Chicago School of Architecture with his visionary thinking and designs, came to Chicago right after the Great Chicago Fire to help shape the city. He left perhaps the biggest mark. He taught Frank Lloyd Wright to be an architect. Criminally, many of his masterpieces have been torn down over the decades in an urban war on beauty. He died penniless living in a cheap hotel, his body in a potter's field somewhere unknown. No matter. He changed the world. He created vast beauty in his lifetime. Tiny chunks of his terra cotta and wrought iron designs are in museums now. Fragments of his epic creations on display, and finally appreciated.

In his career, aside from designing the finest and fanciest for the wealthy of the time, ornate homes and office buildings, banks, storefronts, and department stores, Louis Sullivan also spent copious time designing beautiful economical structures for schools and libraries and modest merchants. These were general plans that people or groups could look at the design options and cost projections, buy the plans, and have it built. As I type this I wonder if his concept wasn't the impetus for the Sears & Roebuck kit houses that were sold from 1908 to around 1941, and still stand today? I have a sneaking suspicion the very high school I attended on the working class south side of Chicago was one of those stock designs. I learned of him just after high school. I was working in downtown Chicago at my first real job and the hours were odd, 4 am to noon or 10 pm to 6 am, so I'd spend time walking through the city looking at stuff while the streets were nearly empty. I was struck by the beauty of some of the buildings I would pass. I began taking photos of them with my film camera. One day I saw a plaque with his name on it and came to learn many of my favorites were designed by the same great man. This was in the 1980s, there was no Internet. I had to ask questions and do research at my local library to learn about him. He's the guy who said "form follows function", but he would be horrified at the ugly boxes and barren designs built today, with that as the likely and grossly misunderstood rallying cry.

The least we can do. The worst foods we can fill up on. The groaning about being physical. That is the world of Bottom Line Thinking. Instead of beautiful department stores to shop in, with knowledgeable sales staff, and durable, quality goods for sale, we now have steel boxes with angry lighting and cheaply made fast fashion. Instead of a nice fitting room with mirrors and comfy seats and benches, we have tiny squares with some security type personnel counting our choices. It's weird how the world has changed in these strange, lesser ways. To me, Bottom Line Thinking is responsible for the disposable and sorrowful world in which we currently dwell.

We should never settle. Doing the least is the absolute worst kind of thinking. It is misery in a can. Anyone suggesting that doing the least is admirable is not your friend. How about just don't do things you don't believe in? Don't work for multinationals, don't invest in the stock market, don't flip houses to "get yours" because that is "how the world works". Only misery worlds work that way. I don't want to feed into that reality, thank you very much. I want durable goods and good work for good pay. I want community that cares, and people doing what they were born to do.

Keep in mind, the government has done plenty of studies of our minds, starting with Dr. Proctor eugenics experiments pre-WWII to remote viewing, to MK ultra. I'm not being a conspiracy nut, we know these things happened. We know the government and universities have studied the depths of our psychic and intuitive abilities. They know how powerful our minds are, and they know what to do to make us act in certain ways.

We are poisoning ourselves with processed food, soda, microwaves, and Teflon. We've lost so much knowledge of building things, or craftsmanship, or about growing food, or navigating by the sky. I was probably 30 when I found out you could make pie filling out of fresh fruit and you didn't have to buy it in cans. I am being serious. I was 13 the first time I saw a peach that wasn't canned in heavy syrup or cubed in fruit cocktail. As a child, my mother's mother probably helped grow the family's food, but she didn't do that in the city. My parents didn't grow any food when I was growing up. I was cut off from the food supply at some point, me and every other urban kid in my socioeconomic group.

I've worked hard to do better. I started growing food shortly after I was married. An elderly couple down the street showed me how to grow flowers one spring and I was off to the races. I am eternally grateful for that gift! Some summers I grew sixty percent or more of our food. We felt great and ate well. My peers, the women I knew, were not into such things at all. They thought it was weird and kind of gross I was out there gardening in the dirt. Some felt my domesticity was too much. I like it when someone who once mocked me for cooking or gardening is now growing stuff in their yard or posting photos of a cake they made from scratch. I don't care to point it out, I'm just happy they found their own way. Growing food is healing. Beyond the food itself, the act of growing and tending to it has given me a sense of peace and well-being similar to a quiet day at a beach. It's celebrating this paradise we are living in.

Today, it is great to see on social media so many young people growing food and canning. Far beyond my own efforts, they are studying herbal medicine and even raising livestock. It has become almost political. It is hard to live our politics. Expensive even. It's a challenge sometimes to get things done without visiting a big box store of some sort. In many communities it's all they have.

My attempts to be healthy have ebbed and flowed, and some times are better than others. Since I became autonomous, I generally eat what I want when I want. Rather than cooking full meals like when I was part of a couple, I snack a lot, or I have smaller meals usually. Not having to eat when I wasn't hungry caused me to drop weight after my husband left, several clothing sizes down in fact. I didn't even realize! Nowadays, if I want a brownie, I have a brownie. If I begin to have a pattern of eating "bad food" for a few weeks I will check in with myself. It's likely I am feeling sad or nervous about some situation in my life. Usually financial.

Recently, I bought a small 'Wild Mikes' brand, frozen pizza for myself, and when I went to put it in the freezer there was already one in there. I wondered how many I'd eaten recently? Was it four, was it six in the last month? Then I opened the crisper to put away a couple avocados only to find my previous avocados had gone bad, and so had a bag of fresh green beans I was so excited to buy but never cooked. I really had to think on it for a day or two. Why was I eating so much processed food yet letting good food rot? It came down to worry I was having about a situation. A judgment was looming over me. I felt like I was chained to some crumbling dark tower dodging falling bricks. Once I identified what was bothering me, I was able to tell myself hurting me with bad food wasn't going to solve my problems, and it was keeping me from feeling and doing my best in body, mind, and spirit.

I got back on doing daily yoga, and demanded I eat healthier. I tried for 70% fruits and veggies. The problem still looms, but I am seeing more ways forward with it. Soon I will untether myself from it. But, I am not harming myself with food or activity, or lack of activity in the meantime. When I start to stress about it, I try to do something healthy, like 5 minutes of yard work, or I'll take the trash out, or scrub the toilet. With that I feel better fast, and I have a sparkly toilet! We all have coping mechanisms. I smoke weed, eat chocolate, and drink too much coffee.

Now more than ever, our actions have repercussions. Not only does falling down drunk look really bad at 60 versus 25, it affects us longer and harder. Right around forty I learned a coke and a candy bar for dinner would result in a hangover just as if I'd drank too much whiskey. Processed sugar is not good for me. I can feel that jagged high, that twitch. I notice too much coffee gives me a twitchy leg at night. Some people call that restless leg syndrome, I know it as Amy drank too much espresso today. It's not a mystery, and I don't need a pill for it.

I have questions; I am not judging, just curious. Do you eat fast food? Do you drink soda, diet or otherwise? How many living fruits and vegetables do you eat in a week? What do you want your end of life to be like?

Certainly tomorrow has no guarantees, but if you are harming yourself with food, liquor, or sloth now, how do you expect it to all play out? When I eat bad, my stomach hurts. Sometimes I poop blood, or all I can do is lay in bed with a hot water bottle on my belly. I don't want to live like that. I like to feel good, not walking around the house holding my gut and canceling plans. If avoiding cheap ass grocery store donuts is the solution, then so be it. Instead of a mediocre daily doughnut, I'll have a nice one or some other pastry once a week. I don't feel slighted - it's quality over quantity. Or as my old Traditional Chinese Doctor Dr. Lee would say, "everything in moderation".

We don't have to turn into fitness gurus, but maybe now, for this part of our life -- The part we owe only to ourselves, maybe here is where we can try to take better care of ourselves, for ourselves? True self care. Maybe it will set a good example for those behind us. Maybe it will give us a better quality of life and a natural end, one without hoses and drugs and breathing apparatuses.

THE END OF THE PERiOD

It's kind of strange that women would lament the end of their period. I mean I get it, if you feel sad about not being able to breed. Turtles can still lay eggs at 100, but they also do zero raising of their offspring. Ever think about that? Every turtle is born alone and when they hatch they know exactly how to be a turtle. But I digress, as I often do.

My first period came on New Year's Eve when I was eleven and a half. My mother, sister, and I were out for pizza with my Aunt Francine and my cousin. I went to the bathroom and there it was. I was excitedly awaiting it, yet it was still a shock when it showed up. I was always asking my mom when was it going to start. She'd ordered a special kit for me a few months before, it came in a pink box with a book all about starting a period and pads in several sizes.

My period was beautiful in its own way, sure, but it was also a lot of cramps, and headaches, and stained underwear. I can remember once in 7th grade blowing out my last pad at school and bleeding all over. I had to walk home, a good eight blocks with my faded jeans visibly full of blood. It was so embarrassing. I think of all the undies I destroyed, the sheets forever stained, mattresses that looked like crime scenes.

Years back, while living in northern Minnesota, I had the great good fortune to befriend an important Native American artist, scholar, and leader, Heart Warrior Chosa. She spoke of a woman's "moon", which I have to admit delighted me. My own cycle nearly always ran with the moon, coinciding usually with the full moon, but sometimes with the new moon, especially during times of change in my life so the reference was an epiphany when she said it.

Heart Warrior also said that in her tribal history, there would be a teepee or hut outside of the tribal area where menstruating women would gather during their moon. They left the tribal village for those days, and spent time alone or together in a camp away from the rest of the tribe as a sacred sort of sabbatical. They would be brought food during that time. She said it was bad to eat food cooked by a menstruating woman, and it was bad luck if she stepped over your clothes, which I can see the practical side of both those things. Ha! This seems like a far better way to experience our period. I wish I had heard about it sooner in life. We all try to push through our days like nothing is going on during that time. It's stupid. We need rest.

I'm not down on the menstrual cycle, but I am down on how it is treated by society here in America. As a young person, I could never understand why we had all these terrible disposable products, many of them scented, that we are or were pressing on the inside of our underwear or worse yet, sticking inside ourselves. When washable reusable pads and collection cups started appearing I was so thankful, but why did it take so long??? Being broke during my marriage, I sometimes had to use a washcloth as a pad because I simply could not afford tampons, and being able to launder and reuse something seemed to make a lot of sense to me. And, yes, I was that broke.

One time in my early 40s I got very sick with rashes and nausea during my period. I was so sick, way more than period problems, but it seemed to subside as soon as my period was over. Then, the next month when my period began, I used a tampon from the same box and those symptoms began to appear almost immediately. It seemed preposterous but not, that the tampon could be the issue. I ran out for a new box and the problems disappeared. It had to be some kind of contaminant in the tampons! Should that really be a surprise? Can we admit it is criminal and by design?

Baby Powder scented, Super-absorbent, space-age polymer, no problem, shove it in - with a new plastic applicator every single time. Sorry to sound crude, but the truth is sometimes painful. Wake up.

This leads back into how lousy women are treated by the modern Medical Industrial Complex. From toxic tampons and scented pads to the fact that most doctors, even female doctors, dismiss any issues related to our periods. I'm sure you or some woman you know had doctors ignore their suffering as mental frailty or overreaction when it was actually a serious illness. Am I wrong? How many of those very illnesses, like ovarian cysts, endometriosis, breast and reproductive organ cancers are caused by the very products we are being sold to soak up our sacred blood? What is super absorbency made from? Is microfiber safe as underpants? Why is there an inch of plastic foam on a majority of bras?

The end of my cycle did feel important. I buried my last tampon in the yard. I honored that part of my life, and I honored the end of that part of my life. However, the end of my period did not take away my womanhood. It is not the end of my importance as a human being, and it is not some melancholy event. Again, that's marketing we have been programmed with for a hundred years.

Think of this: post period, you can wear white anytime without worrying about bleeding through. I will never miss that "whoosh" feeling of my tampon failing, nor the days lost in bed with a hot water bottle because my cramps were so bad, and especially having legitimate anger dismissed because I was "on the rag". Though I suppose no matter what, we are forever the "hysterical female" anytime emotion or emphaticness is shown.

Saying that brings up something interesting. For as sacred as our menstrual cycles are, marking us as givers of life, modern society has used it against us, mocked us for it. Today, we desperately try to ignore this cycle, and that blood-- the very thing that allows us to bring life into the world. Talk about a lead weight of subjugation!

Well I say, no more! Let's work to make all the cycles of the life of women something celebrated again, as there were in the days before Christianity, when people lived by and celebrated the seasons, the earth, and the stars. Let's make sure our daughters, grand-daughters, and great grand-daughters never have to feel shame for the very thing that brought them, and all of us, into the world.

HOT FLASHES & OTHER EXCiTEMENT

Hot flashes: they sound terrifying. They are something women have long been ashamed by and often looked to hide, cover up, and never discuss. Allow me. Menopause is just another stage of life, no better but no worse. Think of it like Puberty #3, there's the Pre-teen Puberty we all know about. There's the "Adult Puberty" of our early 30s-ish, with the realization there is no going back, and now number three, Menopause. Do we call these the crone years, elder-ship, old age? None of that sounds right for me today, which makes "Be The Orca" sound pretty good actually. I might be in my middle fifties, but I feel really alive. This is a great new adventure!

I cannot recall ever seeing my mother have a hot flash. The first time I saw someone have a hot flash was my friend Christine around five years ago. She calmly stated with a funny smile, "I can't even stop it. There's nothing I can do!" I was like "About what?" Puzzled as we sat in my living room having coffee during her visit. I was totally in the dark, then she mildly wiped a sheen from her cheek. She said she was having a hot flash and the statement was the joke she'd make to her partner and son when they occurred at home. I was fascinated. I was still having my period. I'd never witnessed such an amazing thing!

For me, symptoms began with a more sporadic period. The last year it came on the equinoxes and solstices instead of the full moons. Then started the "hot flashes", which were not at all what I expected. At first I didn't even know what it was. The heat came from inside and traveled outward to my skin. For a while mine were absolutely out of control!

Everyone is different, of course, but for me hot flashes felt at first like the warmth that spreads over you when embarrassed, that "weren't her cheeks red?" feeling. In fact it felt very much like embarrassment, traveling from the back of my neck and shoulders over my head to my face in very much the same way. Then it gets hotter, and hotter, times ten, pushing out through my whole body.

It's an actual physiological thing - I can soak through my clothes or my bed sheets in a quick two minutes. I just randomly heat up and begin to sweat profusely. I must go up five degrees, because my lovers feel it; they've marveled at it. My dog will leap from the bed if I have one in the night, and she is usually only at the foot of the bed!

When I first hit menopause, it was a summer with a record heat wave where I live. I laughed to myself about how would I even know if I was having a hot flash in the heat? I learned indeed I could tell the difference!!! Easily, in fact! While I stood in a kiddie pool (my turtle's pool) in the yard I noticed the hot flashes were accompanied by a prickly sensation on the backs of my hands, like the "pins and needles" feeling when a limb falls asleep. Once I figured out that symptom, I could identity them earlier, and figure out what triggered them. Turns out they were not so random.

I'm sure most women will have some of these triggers and some will have others. Weird random things brought them on such as drinking alcohol, spicy food, actually being embarrassed or stressed, any moment of stress in fact, and sex - especially right after, sometimes during.

I tried different things to ease the severity of the hot flashes. I have taken herbs for some of my symptoms such as dong quai and chaste tree, which I also used for PMS during "the period years". Simple things like slowing my breathing and focusing on a slow and controlled in and out breath, even just a few cycles, 15 or 20 seconds of slow controlled breathing have helped a lot. It can stop a hot flash faster than anything else so far. Most times, the person or people I was with didn't notice the momentary change in my breathing. However, had the heat overtaken me, they would certainly have been aware.

Not to say I am ashamed, I take notice of them verbally if it's obvious. I enjoy that it is shocking to acknowledge menopause. I have found younger women and all men are either flustered or fascinated by someone being honest about what is happening during this time. It is so taboo and unspoken. People can talk about all kinds of shocking stuff, but bring up menopause and everything changes, ha! I like to say, "I'm having a warm moment."

I'll remove a layer for a few minutes until it passes, because the other side of the hot flash is freezing a few minutes later! No one talks about that, but much like a fever, or the sweat of a hot day, it's trying to cool our bodies off, and it does, and then I need those layers right back on.

We women keep so much of our menstrual experience secret. So few of us even share about it with our partners, so unfortunately men are in the dark on this whole thing. I don't have any shame about this part of my life; I welcome when people ask me with wonder about it. I am open and honest about my experience. It's what spurred this little book.

Let's face it, there is a lot happening in our bodies all of the time. We are women, givers of life. We are built differently than men, our minds and bodies are different, and we need different things. We spend four decades or so bleeding for a week every month, (I recently heard some 450 periods each), and yet we survive. It is remarkable, really. What amazing things our bodies are, and how incredible this life with all its magic!

Life is an ever changing kaleidoscope of moments, so I will delight in this moment just as I have any other. Yeah, I get down. We all do. Sometimes when it rains it pours -- with disappointment, sorrow, undesired change. Life can be painful, sometimes one bad event spurs another and another. It can feel like the whole world is against us. But we have to pull ourselves back on those darkest of days, to the moment we are in and see the beauty. We have to find joy in the moment, in little things, flowers, the changing seasons, birds chirping.

Suffering is all around us, but so is beauty, love, and kindness. When I was seven, my beloved grandparents died only a few months apart. I was looking for answers. My mother encouraged me to read about death in various world religions since we did not practice any at home but science and wonder. I learned of Buddhism's Four Noble Truths and The Eightfold Path. Even at that young age it made a lot of sense to me. I'd seen suffering all around as a kid, on the streets of downtown Hammond, Indiana, where Vietnam vets in wheelchairs, missing various limbs and battling numerous demons, sat along the street asking for change, or in the fire scorched windows pocking the looming, high-rise housing projects off the highway. My father was a fireman in Calumet City, on the south side of Chicago. Human suffering came home with him on many long days.

To live is to suffer, but is that a bad thing? We suffer from connectedness or attachment, and when it is broken through loss. Maybe we would not suffer had we not loved, but isn't that worse suffering?

Once we accept that life isn't going to be perfect, we can go a long way toward happiness. And what does that have to do with hot flashes? A surprising lot! As I sometimes chant around the house when shit goes bad,

"Control your fear and persevere!"

Let's revisit that breathing thing again. Much of the mitigation of hot flashes is in controlling our breathing, and it's the same in times of stress. Breath in for three seconds, hold for three seconds, on the exhale try for six seconds. Do it twice, three times. See how it feels. Try it for a minute, then three, five, ten. With a bit of controlled breathing I can usually stop a hot flash. Proper breathing will help you master yourself and your emotions, and it gives you time to stop a stress reaction.

Focus on your breathing for three minutes or more - now you are meditating! It's really that easy. Stress kills. It's arguably the biggest killer in the western world, and we've already outlived a lot of people. Controlling our breath and our emotions will go a long way toward good health and longevity.

TO ESTROGEN OR NOT TO ESTROGEN? THAT IS THE QUESTION

When my mother began to prepare for her "change of life" in the 1980s, she turned to books, as an avid reader and library regular. She read about how the pharmaceutical companies kept horses constantly pregnant and hooked up to catheters to take their urine for estrogen production, so women can continue to menstruate and postpone the symptoms of menopause. She was outraged! Why torture an animal to postpone the inevitable? That was her feeling and decision. My mother was vehemently against it and I guess I followed suit in my own time, but what is right for another is not for me to say. You have to do what is right for you.

An old school friend contacted me recently. She is going through an unexpected divorce, and with my own experience being so extreme, sometimes people contact me for encouragement. I am glad to be there for her or anyone. The more of that shit I can spin into gold, the better! Please let my bad experience help you!

In her case, her husband just handed her divorce papers out of the blue! With all she was going through, plus working full-time, and the passing of a dear friend. In addition to packing and moving, and all the rest that life brings, she told me point blank, she needed the estrogen. She simply couldn't afford the hot flashes and all of it at the same time she was dealing with her heartbreak and so much change. That made perfect sense to me. She was doing what she knew she needed to do for herself. I was happy to hear it. No two of us are the same. I'm not here to judge anyone, I'm here to live my life.

I'm not down on estrogen if it's right for you. Nor am I down on Botox, filler, or face lifts. However, if we cling to these false symbols of beauty, youth culture, or trying to avoid aging, we are beholden to being mere eye candy. From today to our great, great grand daughters, we are keeping the weight on their back to be some impossible perfection, some forever young beauty. Perfection. Yet, it is so absurd, all of us are already perfection. How is any sparrow in the tree less than perfect?

How I wish I'd realized that sooner, that I was always perfectly me. As you are perfectly you. Of course I am always striving for better, that is part of being alive. My greatest wish is for all children, all people to know they are perfect as they are. There would be no more war, no hate, no crime. Everything would change.

When my own long marriage ended suddenly, my husband taunted me with messages and emails calling me things like "the faded dish". As if after a quarter century together, his love of me had never gone deeper than my skin? That was maybe the most shocking part of it, that all our projects, all my hard work, all our long talks over coffee didn't matter, just that my face remained agreeable enough.

This concept still lives strong today. It's hard to break. This idea that we women are supposed to home make, work a gig, and always look like a supermodel. I read an article some years ago, an interview with a famous actress and sex symbol of the 1970s and '80s. At the time of the interview it was probably twenty years after that. She still did appearances on TV shows and in movies and commercials, and was still very attractive. Yet in the interview, she said she was married to a younger man and she never lets him see her without a full face of makeup. It was one of the saddest statements I ever read.

Yes, we all want to look good and be attractive, but what's attractive at 18 is different than at 25, 35, 50, or 72. Let's look our best, and let's do our best, but for ourselves, in the way best for us. Stop bowing to society's fickle standard of beauty. Beauty comes from the inside out - like a hot flash! It burns our skin based on how we feel inside.

The uniqueness of each of our bodies is what makes humanity beautiful. Any body issues I've ever had have been the words of others or other people measuring me against someone else. Now I understand those were not my issues but theirs. I remind myself all bodies are beautiful, even divine, including mine.

Instead of estrogen, I switched from coconut/almond milk to unsweetened organic soy milk to potentially help with a boost of plant estrogen. I would drink four ounces a day, in addition to using it with cereal or oatmeal, and it seemed to lessen the hot flashes over all. I know soy is also controversial, and some people say use fermented soy only. Whatever, I don't know, I can only say what helped me, and certainly it could be a placebo effect.

About a year ago, I got into a conversation at the grocery store with two young gentlemen about all the variety of "milks" now available. I said I switched to soy for the protein and to help my hot flashes.

One of the young men nodded. "That's what my mother did, for exactly that reason, and she's a doctor!"

"Really?" I was excited. This was just a "Crazy Amy Theory" I'd come up with. I figured even as a placebo effect it would help if I believed. But I was right for real! Great news! We all laughed.

Back to Heart Warrior Chosa: she also told me that in her entire life, she had never needed deodorant until she hit menopause. I asked her to explain why. She explained that a woman's moon acted as a cleansing for her, and since she had reached menopause she no longer had that monthly cleansing. I asked, "What about men? They don't have a monthly cleansing either?" She agreed and said that was why men do not live as long as women, and why men do sweat lodges. In fact, she said, only post-menopausal women were allowed inside the sweat lodge.

I'd forgotten the idea that the sweat lodge was the male version of cleansing the inside of the body until I was invited to an inipi last year, and in reading up on the rules, there was a large disclaimer that menstruating women were not allowed on the property during the lodge. "Oh yeah", I said to myself. It seems maybe sexist at first, but the menstruating woman is already in a process of release, sweat lodge might be too much, and it explains why elder women are allowed to sweat lodge, because we no longer have that monthly cleansing.

If I was cleansing my body every month when my "moon" came, then a hot flash is perhaps the replacement of this monthly cleansing. If my body is releasing toxins in a new way, then I don't necessarily want to hinder that release. It used to be said that hormone replacement therapy caused breast cancer. I wonder if that was from a build-up of toxins that the hot flashes would have otherwise released? But then again, I believe in most cases we could cure all of our own illnesses if we just tried.

The loss of strength is just part of aging, but can be delayed and diminished greatly by taking care of ourselves and being active. Walks in nature! I cannot recommend anything more than walks in nature, whatever you are comfortable with. I'm not talking about distance hikes or free soloing Yosemite, (of course I'm not saying not to do those things either). I'm saying stay active and engaged. Try new things. Take on new activities. If you can't be on the tennis team anymore, teach tennis at the park district. You'll still play every day. If exhaustive sports are part of your life, find new ways to enjoy them, or try a different sport, maybe martial arts.

Years ago, I used to live in the Bridgeport neighborhood of Chicago and I'd walk my dog all around. Sometimes in the morning we'd catch a tai chi group in the park. It was an amazing group of forty or fifty Chinese people, all moving in unison. Standing on one foot for extended periods with their arms outstretched. Sometimes we sat on a bench in the distance to watch in awe. It was amazing, barely 7am, and all the people appeared to be 70, 80, 90, maybe some over 100 performing effortlessly feats I could not easily replicate at that time. There's a lot we can do to stay nimble and spry.

SEX AND MENOPAUSE

When I got here, I knew very little about menopause, and even less about sex and menopause. In movies and on TV older women were always either frigid, or lonely and sex crazed, or the "long suffering", dutiful wife. I'd noticed lube ads like KY Jelly seemed to use imagery of older women, as if to say when you get old, you get dry. There were not a lot of positive images of sexy older women. Given all that, I was not feeling optimistic.

Then there was the other thing I was dealing with: my husband walking out of my life and into my nightmares with months of vile messages. I believed his insults and slurs. I didn't think I would ever have sex again.

If I was all those terrible things, all old and ugly, who would ever have sex with me? Would I have to pay for sex? How does one even do that? I had a job at the time, I was earning okay money, but not "buy sex" money. What does something like that cost? Where do you go? Did this mean I would I be lonely from now on? I was terrified!

Though my marriage was far from perfect, we always slept cuddled together, and we very seldom went more than a few days without intimacy. There were never separate bedrooms. I was never not in the mood. If anything I was usually turned down. I enjoy sex. It was not a weapon I used. It was not something I used to catch a guy and then ignore him. I love sex. The prospect of never having sex again was devastating.

These ideas of losing my sex drive, of needing lube, of no one ever wanting to have sex with me again were haunting me. I was mortified. Then in a meditation, I had the realization that it was simply marketing.

I believe most of the symptoms we experience or have been told we will experience are lies. The whole lack of libido and the drying out of our vaginal cavity, lies. I think it's marketing created by corporations selling cures. The lack of libido may be true for some, but not for all. Ask yourself if that is real or dictated? Question even your own beliefs. Are they real, or are they what you were told through popular culture, media, and marketing? Many women say their libido disappears but I believe this to be a societal falsity.

Perhaps women feel unattractive when menopause hits because it is a symbol of "old" and that self-consciousness is what creates a lower sex drive. I'm only halfway through my fifties, but I have noticed no lack, and perhaps even a brighter and bigger drive for sex. If it is up to me, that will never change.

When I accepted that, the desperate look on my face must have disappeared, because I will tell you right now, I have had plenty of interest from men, both older and younger. Beauty, as I've said, is exuded with a smile.

Maybe if we weren't so stressed about our bodies and our looks and measuring up, and now getting old, we'd be a lot wetter down there, and our sex drive would resurface, and interest in us from our partner or partners would grow? Not to say these things are always related, we are all different.

In the months after my breakup, I got back in contact with some old friends. One, an old friend from grade school, said she'd gone through menopause already. She said she'd totally lost her sex drive since she hit menopause. WHAT????!?!?! I asked questions, probably more than I should have to try to understand what exactly was hampering her desires. She always had many boyfriends over the years. She was talking about how great sex was while I was still a virgin. In the end, it seemed almost like her lack of sex drive was because that was what she had been told. Marketing strikes again!

Now I'm talking vaginal sex here, not anal sex in regard to lube. Please know, I am not knocking lube in any way. If you need it, you like it, or you prefer it, go all in with it. Pleasure is about where you find it, not where I find it. I use lube when I masturbate. A dry vagina is easily fixed with a little lube. It's as simple as that - there is no reason for anyone to deny themselves pleasure for something so easily resolved.

But is that all physical or is it psychological? I'm gonna overshare right here. For me, I have never really "needed" lube but once in my life, and while it was fairly recently, it had nothing to do with menopause.

Too Much Information Alert! Someone I was involved with hurt my feelings deeply, but beyond that, they did it on purpose to hurt my feelings! Why would anyone be purposefully mean to someone they claim to like? It's weird. Every time I tried to get to the bottom of it, they kept denying they were acting mean. Later, they admitted they were being mean and blamed some perceived slight they refused to talk about as justification for their actions.

Once I understood what had happened, my newly discovered self love and real boundaries caused my nether region to refuse to cooperate. The result was I could not get excited by this person at all. It wasn't menopausal dryness; it was cognitive dissonance. It took me weeks, if not months, to work through that whole thing. I had to really step back and look at the situation and the relationship.

Having issues and exploring them through bondage with another consenting adult to work them out is one thing. It's a great thing! Being mean to hurt someone's feelings is something I will likely never understand, thankfully. If someone makes you feel bad during sex or after sex, don't waste your time with them. Know they have something they need to work through. If you like them, maybe talk to them about it, and urge them to seek help, but stay away. Avoid anyone who wants to harm you.

It's sad, but here in America we are still really sexually repressed. I am always shocked to hear how many couples have sexual issues of some sort. Everyone's sex drive is different. This is important to consider, albeit a little late to say now at menopause, but we have physical needs as humans. It's important to have a partner we share a good sexual balance with. Studies show we need 12 hugs a day to thrive as humans. Affection is important and needs to be tended to. Everyone needs and deserves love; what that is remains different for each of us.

Let's get away from extremes and negatives and back to the fun stuff. Sex...

If someone is attracted to you enough to want to fuck you, there is no reason to be self-conscious about your body or your pleasure. Go full abandon! Release some good for you hormones and brain chemicals!!! Love is a drug - enjoy it. Revel in it. Never feel ashamed about how you look. We are all beautiful in our own way! That is not cliche at all. Most people are only as unattractive as they feel. A smile does make all the difference. Confidence is what beauty truly is. For me, I feel freer sexually now more than ever!

The time for self-consciousness for all of us should be over -- All women! Models are paid thousands to successfully portray confidence in the most outlandish of fashions, I'm sure there are plenty of times they want to burst out laughing at the ridiculous attire they are strutting around in. If they can pull that off, surely any of us in our birthday suit, enjoying pleasure, should feel equally confident, and be ready to burst out laughing too. Sex is fun. Don't hold back, don't try to cover yourself. Be Free! Enjoy some wild abandon! If not now, when???

Of course, again, we are not all the same. Some people honestly just don't enjoy sex, and that's okay. It's okay to have only platonic friendships. It's okay if you really aren't into it, just don't let fear, or trauma, or self-consciousness put those feelings on you. Make sure it's genuine. If you truly aren't into having sex with a partner ever, or again, understood. But maybe find ways to pleasure yourself? Does asexuality include masturbation or not? I would imagine some do, some don't. Those that do, single people, and those who are partnered, all people should be able to pleasure themselves...

LOVE YOURSELF! SELF-PLEASURE IS BEAUTIFUL

Feeling pleasure is vital. If you haven't enjoyed much sexual self-pleasure before, maybe now is the time! If you need some lube, get some, use it up, rub yourself, explore. It's heartbreaking to say this in writing of menopause, but I must, this is America.

There is no shame in masturbation. How can someone else please us if we cannot please ourselves? For too long we have been told good girls don't like sex, and so many girls and boys have been told masturbation is bad. Those are some of the worst crimes I can think of. It's utter nonsense, it is also dangerous on a societal scale. When natural actions and normal human functions are called "bad" it causes us twitches, mutations, and perversions.

If you don't enjoy sexual pleasure because of something bad that has happened to you, perhaps now is the time and self-pleasure is a way to work that out. You don't want to leave this vessel without appreciating pleasure. I'm not suggesting going against your natural sexuality if you are asexual, but the rest of us who crave pleasure should definitely be able to enjoy it and come to understand how to give it to ourselves. It's not dirty. It is beautiful.

I came late to masturbation, or rather, I came late to embracing masturbation. I used to always say, "I'd rather have sex than masturbate". However, in recent years, a friend helped me see the beauty of loving ourselves, not as a shameful or second-rate option, but as the exaltation it is and should be! To be able to love and satisfy oneself is part of self-mastery, and is as important and special as meditation or a long bath after a hard day.

If we incorporate that self-mastery into practice with positive intent, well my friends, that is magic in its simplest and most powerful form! (Side note, imagine your goals in meditation, and also in masturbation! You can make it so. We should never stop practicing this magic. We can keep harnessing our sexual energy to reach the goals we are striving toward forever.)

Life is too short and too long for longing. I'm not suggesting we will need to service ourselves because we cannot otherwise get laid, rather so we can be better partners in getting laid. By knowing and showing your partner how to better please you, but also to explore our own pleasure, our own bodies.

Improving on self-pleasure can add spice to an existing relationship, and make new relationships better from the start. Or if it's all auto-erotica, then we should definitely know how to give ourselves pleasure! Just those words, "explore our own pleasure" makes me feel a little tingly, like what would that be like? What could I still find? I think I want to explore more. How high can we go?

DON'T FAKE IT TiLL YOU MAKE IT

I'm just going to add this right here. If you are one of my sisters who has spent their sexual life faking orgasms, I ask why?

Why? WHY? Shame on you! And, I apologize for admonishing you. It's probably not your fault.

For all the harm that practice causes to society, the worst suffering is certainly your own. I feel bad - that lack of satisfaction makes my heart hurt for you. Life is about joy and pleasure! If you are asexual, then joyfully be that, be joyfully whatever you are, but please don't pretend.

By faking, not only have you let all the rest of us down, but you let all of your partners down, because you were too afraid to say "more of that", or "a little to the left". You let men off the hook as far as actually learning how to please you properly. Sadly, you failed as a teacher in the subject of you. By being afraid to say what you want, maybe you don't even know, but by faking orgasms you made each of us who are actually wanting to have a real orgasm feel like we are asking too much.

In the end, you didn't do yourself or the world any favors. You are sexually unfulfilled and your partner either knows deep down you were faking and this has hurt their confidence, or they believed you, and therefore saw no reason to edge up or try something different. PLEASE stop faking orgasms, it does a disservice to all of us. Just say if you are too tired or not in the mood, or find a way to let the mood find you. Is that so bad?

I say you let men off the hook because they are not women and therefore need to be shown how our bodies work, and what feels good. Each of us is obligated to teach our partners what we like, or to explore and find out if we don't know. That is how it should be with a relationship based in friendship. (Please note, I say men because I'd imagine a lesbian couple would have a more innate understanding of each other's bodies, but this is my ignorance as a heterosexual. I have been told, by some of my homosexual brothers and sisters, that the sex between same sex couples is more informed and more easily pleasurable from the simple familiarity of how the equipment works and feels. But of course a partner of any gender can be satisfying or not.) Satisfaction, REAL satisfaction, is about taking our time, exploring our bodies, and feeling comfortable with our intimacy.

Can we make a deal? Don't let the lights go out on your ecstasy. Please don't.

Faking an orgasm is lying in the worst of ways. Sex should not be a chore, if you don't like sex, don't want sex, or aren't into it, just say so. For me, there have been times sex felt like a chore, or I've been too tired to give it my all, but that is the exception. I always try to make the best of it, to relax and enjoy the moment. I have faked an orgasm a couple times. I didn't like it at all, it felt weird. Foolish, and like I was a liar. I can have great sex and not have an orgasm, it's still a really good time. Sometimes I can have an orgasm with just a few little rubs. Depends on the moment, the day, the partner.

I don't need to pretend with fake orgasm theatrics. I like sex, with an orgasm or without, it's usually a good time no matter what. Yeah I want an orgasm, damn right, but it's not always there. Sometimes because I was having a hard time asking for what I needed. I get it, it's hard to say, "like this, not like that", but then I realized, men do that all the time. They tell us what they want - harder, slower, just the tip, whatever, so I decided to do the same. Turns out most men are thankful for the direction.

I read once about how ancient tribal cultures had sex purely for pleasure. They believed pregnancy came from the gods, not from the intercourse they were having; that was all just for fun, or love, or pleasure. In many ways they were correct.

I have a squirrel family that lives in the tree in my front yard. I learn a lot from those squirrels. One day I opened the curtains to see two mating on the fence. The male saw the movement of the curtain and looked over as if to say, "Do you mind?" I quickly looked away so they could finish without me being a spectator. I was a little embarrassed. They didn't seem to miss a beat. A few months later, they had their adorable babies. Life is pretty simple. Sex and pleasure are part of it. But we lose sight of that all the time.

We in the western world are a mess of puritanical holdovers from the religious zealots and kooks who got sent over to America. We are a land of "celibate" priests who usually are not very celibate at all, and often in the grossest of ways. We have gotten far from our biological need for pleasure and instead we do all these weird things based on a society that has forgotten nature's laws for the often foolish man's laws. Especially in regard to societal norms of the current era.

What a mess. What a flaming pile of nonsense. Faking orgasms, fear of self pleasure, using consumerism to pacify our unquenched sex drive. How did we get to a world where women fake pleasure? That, maybe more than anything, says "failed society". I say no more. Please Stop! Learn what gives you pleasure and share it with your partner. Life is short; please, please, please take care of your needs.

EMOTiONAL OUTBURSTS

Recently, I've seen and heard older women blaming menopause for their emotional outbursts. In the western world, for a couple hundred years now, any woman who is angry, outspoken, passionate, or strong willed has been called "hysterical". It is considered bad form for any woman to get angry. Today, Joan Of Arc would be medicated and told to cheer up. Her shrink might report she had illusions of grandeur in her file.

What if menopause is not the reason for your emotional outburst of anger or sorrow? What if you are totally justified and proper in those feelings? Perhaps we are just fed up with the unjust power structure, the war machine, the absurd work week, and the nearly impossible struggle most of us face to just survive. Then we reach this age, and we can no longer live quietly suffering in this mad world.

Women are so quick to ignore their feelings, to discount their intuition. We are taught to believe that a desire to achieve our own goals and dreams is selfish. We're taught to ignore or medicate away feelings of unfulfilledness, but it does not make them wrong. Unfulfilledness, that's a mouthful. We drink to forget, so to speak. Alcohol, anti-depressants and other pharma, weed, hard drugs, sex, hoarding, junk food, or even exercise. There is likely something we do or have done to excess to cover up or fill the hole left by whatever we had to stand aside for, be it family, children, spouse, or career.

Not that I drink much. I drank more in high school and before I was 21 than all the alcohol I have consumed as an adult. And, I will not apologize for it. I question what came first, my partying, or the realization that there is a lot of ugliness and horror in the world that I wasn't prepared for? There is so much unnecessary suffering. Ask a million stoner kids why they are getting high, and I bet at the core is the broken system, the broken family, and the lack of real opportunity. Why do we self-medicate? Because the world we live in is insane. At least it is if we watch the news or scroll the Internet. The sky is falling. The sky is always falling. Forever.

In America, we are expected to work until 62, 65, now 67. I want to say things have never been like this before, but man's inhumanity to man has sadly gone on for all of recorded history.

This is a new place in life for us, we are crossing a threshold. For myself, and I assume for others, there is a gnawing desire to push. A frantic need to accomplish, and/or a sense of betrayal of ourselves for what we didn't achieve. While I have "no regrets", I am surprised I landed at this point in life so suddenly. It seems like just yesterday I was 30. Somewhere in the back of my head, I had this notion that I could go back and redo some of the years, but of course that cannot be.

I spent years, okay maybe decades, smiling through other people's bad choices, denying my often accurate intuition, and accepting "my place" in the world. So I ask: how many times in life have you piped down over some decision at your job or by someone in your life, only to have been correct? I bet if you were honest, a lot. We are told to discount our intuition, our true dreams, our individuality, for our entire life. Now that we reach the fourth quarter, we are mad as hell. Rightfully so, and we just won't take it anymore!

The "hysterical woman" is the constant derision of society, our families, and so on. Being emphatic is being unreasonable. Yet we as a society worship that same passion and will in our male artists. If Salvador Dali or Pablo Picasso or Jim Morrison have strong emotions or intuitive feelings they are placed on a pedestal as gods in man's clothes, but if you or I point out the very same thing, we are disrespected, unheard or ignored, marked as "impossible" or "crazy".

We all know about difficult actresses and singers. We call them Divas, but are they really? And if so, how did they get that way? Is it the frustration of always having to fight for a place at the table, even when they are the golden goose?

We must be seen and not heard. We have been taught to stand aside, stand back, and that our emotions are too much. We are forever dismissed.

If we stand firm, we are a bitch. If we have opinions, they are less valid than others. Men and women are different and the same; our differences are important, they are beautiful! The fact that we have lost our power in the modern world is by design, it is the anti-feminine stance of Western Society. We act as though we are sophisticated and modern because we don't have clitoridectomies, but this world has gone mad because the power of the feminine is constantly denied. It continues to be quelled.

We give all attention to the masculine, the brute strength, the might is right. This is why our society is a mess. This is why there is so much war and destruction. We need to heal ourselves and take the helm as the equal, or we are forever doomed. Not just you and me, but all of us, and more generations. Standing back will no longer serve our legacy, nor society, nor generations to come.

Take this time as the gift it is! Use it to create a new world around you! Stop being brushed aside. If a hysterical woman we need to be, then hysterical women we will be! If that's what will stop the poisoning of the planet and our food, if it will repair the future of humanity, count me in! It is time we embrace our strong emotions and quit allowing them to be blamed on our womanhood, our period, and now menopause. Stand and affirm - you are important! You are the most important person in your life, and if you are not, you are in error. For how can we help our loved ones if we cannot stand up for ourselves?

It's a man's world, but that is because we have allowed it to be. We have been subjugated for so long we don't even remember the power we held. History for so long called the Vikings heathens, but in Viking days women were equal to men; they were understood as half of the equation of life. Tribal cultures called savage yet they appreciated and celebrated the masculine and feminine as separate but equal in power. Somehow via Christianity and the other Abrahamic religions, as practiced in the so-called modern world, women are lesser. That is by design. I can only speculate the reason, but the result has been the destruction of the planet, the diminishment of the family, and every manner of devastation perpetuated by this subjugation, from farming to medicine and education, things are a mess.

We can break this cycle! We owe it to ourselves and all the daughters ahead, ours or not, to stop the madness. If it takes getting mad, standing tall in the face of suffering, and having an "emotional outburst", so be it!

SECURITY IS A HOAX

If there is one lesson I have learned in life, it is that security is a giant hoax society sells us all on, but does not exist. At least it does not exist externally. We are told our whole lives that we need to find a secure career in a "good" field, and we need to go to school to prepare for these things. Society tells us to find security in a good partnership, in true love, in family. Security will protect us we are told when we install an alarm system. Security "they" say, comes from a fortified border, a brick house that the big bad wolf cannot blow down, in bells, whistles, and cameras that watch us.

The truth is a different matter.

There is no security in a job or even a career; these thing can become obsolete in a day. One new discovery can and has rendered entire industries to dust. Security doesn't come from any job. They can replace you tomorrow. Even if they can't, they can. I remember working with a woman who did an incredible amount of work. She was a dedicated employee, giving it her all every day, and they just fired her one day. Some middle management guy didn't like her no nonsense attitude and made a fuss. It took four, five, maybe six people to replace her in the end. You'd think they would have sent her flowers and offered her a big raise when they realized, but no. Companies will seldom admit if they make a mistake like that.

Security does not come from fortified walls or alarm systems. They can be scaled, destroyed, and rendered easily useless. If someone wants what you have, if they want to harm you, they will find a way to do that. A camera can let you watch your house get robbed while at your job, or perhaps it can spy on you for others. And what happens in a blackout?

Security does not come from a relationship. Your partner could be lying to you right now. They could disappear into the night. They could be plotting your death though of course I certainly hope not. Even in a truly committed relationship, they can drop dead on you. Then what?

The only security we have in this life is within us, within ourselves. This is a secret no one wants us to know. That's why such inner insecurity is bred, it is bred within us via media and societal standards that are absurd. No one is ever pretty enough, muscular enough, or smart enough. They keep us in a state of constant insecurity by telling us what we are supposed to be, how we are supposed to feel inside, and how we are supposed to look.

Anything beyond that thin scope is wrong we are told. If we find ourselves attracted to chunky people, or someone of the same sex as us, we are told we are sick. If we are happy without great wealth, we are lazy. If we live in a trailer, we are trash. But these things are not true. None of those things matter. We are a vast spectrum of beings. That is what creates security for us, our variety and multitude. Science shows, biologically, socially and in physics, the security of our continuation comes from our variety - that makes our individuality vital!

That means security can only be found in acceptance and pursuit of what we are passionate about individually, what we are good at, and what we wish to do. Security is in self-love, self-acceptance, and self-friendship. There is no place outside of ourselves where we can find true security.

Security is a state of being, not a mindless protectionism. That kind of thinking just puts us in a self created prison afraid of our fellow man. Security can only come from inside ourselves, much like happiness can only come from inside our self. And to be honest, they are very similar in reality.

Security and happiness are partners when it comes to living in joy. They are seeds that grow within us individually and they must be nurtured.

No one is secure all of the time, just like no one is happy all of the time, but we can spend most of our time in these states if we just allow ourselves. Accept that the only person you can really count on in life is you. That is a wonderful thing, an important thing, to be reliable for ourselves, to show up for ourself.

If this sounds scary, understand that forgetting it is much scarier. When we count too much on other people, the government, the church, our family, our friends and partners, we push them away or we become dependent on them. Or worse yet, we show them all the ways to hurt us if they happen to have sadistic or wicked tendencies.

Accepting and understanding that all we have is ourselves is true freedom. When we accept we are it, we are born and die with ourselves, it opens us up to freedom and independence. We understand a job is a means to an end, but we cannot depend on it. We can only depend on ourselves. We all want to stand on our own two feet. Self-reliance is part of thriving.

When we accept that we can only depend on ourselves in a romantic relationship, jealousy and fear of abandonment have no place within us. We want people in our life, but we don't need them. Need is debt, and there is no security there. Of course we all want the support of others around us, "no man is an island" as the saying goes, but once we've passed the age of dependency, which biologically is 14, then the rest is up to us!!

That is why choosing our own path is vital. If you love numbers but are working as a cashier, push through and learn the skills that will bring you joy and earn a handsome living. If you are a great composer, then do so, and seek out people to support your vision. If you are a natural healer, or a natural gardener, or can tell a great story, these are important skills! If wood just feels good in your hand and you like to make things, learn all you can about the varied aspects of woodworking until you find your niche.

When I was a kid, I declared all people were prodigies and geniuses at something, but too many never figure out at what. We have to keep on trying different things - all kinds of things - until we figure it out. If you have never figured it out, don't stop trying now! This is what life is about. This is where true security is built.

The swallow does not try to be an eagle, and an eagle could not be a swallow; they are completely different because they are born to behave in their own particular way. Security only comes from learning who we are and being that fully.

It took me a long time to realize the important wisdom that security will never come from a job, a place, a bank balance, nor a relationship. Security, true security comes from one place and one place only, and that is from inside of ourselves. It sounds like some new age BS, but it is not.

FEAR OF CHANGE, SECURITY, AND OUR PATH

As women, we are told to put others first all of the time. We are told our parents, our siblings, our partners, and children especially, often even our coworkers come before us. Think of how many traditional female positions are support.

There is no security in sacrifice, it becomes martyrdom. When we live our lives for others, we serve no one. If you are saying, "that's not what the bible says", then I'll ask you: do you know what the bible says, really? Seems like there's a lot of conflicting information getting tossed around from inside it, it's been that way my entire life. The bible was hand transcribed by monks for hundreds of years under the thumb of various political and religious leaders. It is a book that has been altered, edited, and reinterpreted for the benefit of various kings or popes or powerful whomever.

Beyond all that, there is a clear difference between living your life in the Lord's service and giving up your hopes and dreams to follow a path someone else laid out for you. The two are NOT the same!

You live your life for Jesus, Allah, Satan, or whoever by following your dreams and goals! Why? Because we are all on a different path, and that path is divine for each of us. If you are a composer and you are not throwing yourself 100% into that, you are not putting your god first. Your god, the divine, or whatever one chooses to call it, is what gives us that path. If we fail to follow the calling, then we are living for a paycheck, not for divinity.

If you put your spouse's and children's whims above your calling and your path, you are serving wickedness and decay. There is nothing holy about denying what your true life's purpose is about. If you are a materialistic person, if you are living on the hamster wheel of work life, you've been tricked. That is not what life is. This is all over in the blink of an eye! Life is about so much more than empty consumerism. There is no security in stuff. No handbag is going to feed your soul.

If you devote your life to your partner and your children, your partner can drop dead tomorrow, or leave you, or lose their mind. Your children can take off for their own life's adventures, maybe never to be seen again. Are you going to be angry at these things? Are you going to try to trick your loved ones with manipulation to keep them close? That is not love, and that is certainly not security.

Security is inside you, nowhere else, just inside you. Where? In your heart and your mind, in your body and your soul. All we have is ourselves. Our purpose is our security, it cannot be overstated.

I once had the great privilege of working for nearly a year with two world renowned chefs. Nanci Main and Jimella Lucas are culinary pioneers. They basically created the food scene of Oregon and Washington in the early 1980s. They started the trend of serving locally sourced food, grown, foraged, and caught. They still kept a garden behind their small "retirement" restaurant when I worked as their fill-in baker, while their regular baker was on maternity leave.

In fact, they were the inspiration behind the James Beard Awards so coveted by chefs today. He had heard stories of the two young women chefs on the NW coast serving only local cuisine - fish, crab, mushrooms, berries, all grown or foraged in their community, and he drove over an hour to see for himself. He was enthralled. He took them under his wing, and even wrote the introduction to their first cookbook. They once cooked at the White House for the Clintons. Instead of pursuing a TV cooking show, they started a cooking program with the local elementary school, and helped create a summer camp for kids who were sexually assaulted.

Ever hear the saying, "if you want something done ask a busy person"? That was them; even when I worked for them in their semi-retirement they were spitfires! They were grounded in improving their community.

They were culinary stars by following their path. They lived for what drove them. They changed so many lives! When Jimella was very ill, they held a Celebration of Life for her, one that she was able to attend! It was the most beautiful experience! Hundreds of us attended.

Many people stood up and told stories of coming to their restaurant to cook as school kids and now they were chefs in some of the grandest places in the Pacific Northwest. Or about working for them and learning so much. People had story after story of their generosity and ingenuity, and even though most people in the culinary world of today have no idea about them because they were not on TV. But the people they touched, whose lives they changed, will never forget them. I for one, will never forget them.

Creating the best food they possibly could was their passion. They treated every lunch service like brain surgery; their care and precision was remarkable. Jimella once had me watch her dismember a six foot long sturgeon. She showed me with true devotion every part of the fish and explained how it was prehistoric, and how long they live. She'd even spent time on fishing boats catching them in order to know the sturgeon. She arguably made the best sturgeon dishes on earth. It was because she was following her path. Nanci and Jimella's path gave them security, and great success.

People lose everything in disasters all the time. One person is devastated and falls apart, never to be whole again. Another person mourns what they lost and moves on, knowing things are things and life is precious, and they WILL live to feel joy again. They know, (even if they don't know in words, they know in their subconscious), they are alive, and that is the only security they have or need.

"It's not what happens to you, it's how you deal with it." Those words from my former colleague, again echoing in my head. These are such true words! How we deal with what life throws at us defines our character. It's about resiliency and determination. It's about not losing sight of what is important. It's back to that path. We all get into the weeds sometimes in life. Even the best laid plans go awry, or there have been times in life when we've let happenstance rule or guide us, like an oar-less canoe floating where the current takes us.

There are the times we get on the path of another for a period of time, for a larger vision or project, but we can't live on another's path. Sometimes we take a side path and get completely lost in the woods of life. Sometimes we get disillusioned or hopeless, or we start cutting a new path that isn't really ours either, or we just lie down in the weeds. And sometimes, our vision demands we push forward to make something happen, something we are destined to do. I have been in every one of those scenarios in this lifetime.

We come into this world with no possessions, no past or future, and when we leave this world, we cannot take anything with us. So all of our things are just passing through our hands. The house I live in was built in 1928; it has had numerous owners and will have more to come. Furniture I have loved and left has its own life. Change is all around us.

Change is met with eager excitement early in our lives; we embrace change, growing and changing, learning and advancing in school. We can see change as continuous, it's part of the process getting us to "adulthood": that imaginary place where we have all the answers, that place we always think we'll get to.

But then, around our thirties, we are told to acquire things to maintain - a career, a house, a partner, stuff, and we are supposed to hold tight to these things, and not welcome change as we had before. But are we supposed to hold tight to those things, or are they weights slowly suffocating us, like an orca tangled in a lost fishing net?

It's a strange turnaround in our views on change. Now that we have a house, partner, kids, we don't want them to change schools mid year. We try to make change easy for them, we tell ourselves, but that stability isn't really for them, it is for us. Children are experiencing change every day, just as we did, yet we use protecting them from change as a reason to avoid change. That is our own fear of change, our need to maintain and protect all that we now have. It's control. It's absurd if you think about it.

Now I am not proposing we give up all of our possessions and roam the world in a van, (of course, I'm not not suggesting that either). Can there be a comfortable place in between where we can love the people and things in our lives but not be attached to maintaining them in a way that does harm?

If we don't treat change as a wondrous part of living, then when the inevitability of change comes into our lives in the form of moving, divorce, job loss, empty nesting, or starting over, instead of the eager anticipation we used to look at change with as children, we now we look at those events as negative or bad times. We act in fear. This causes the worst to happen, one event of change kicks off a series of bad actions or events because now we fear change. We went against natural law, nature won, and now we are upset about it. Funny how that is.

We can be so change averse, to our detriment. I have never been outside of America. I am from an upper low-class, or working class, socioeconomic background, so I can only speak of American culture. But, I have seen a lot of this nation and spent time with people of many walks of life.

People who fear change are dangerous. They will hold fast to a sinking ship avoid change, and demand you do too. Yet change is an inevitable part of life. We watch day turn to night and back again. Many of us experience the seasonal changes of winter into summer and spring into fall. So why are we so afraid to leave a job we no longer find rewarding or interesting? By now you might be counting the days to retire from such a job. Okay, but are you making plans for the change that comes when that day arrives?

We girls were raised on living "happily ever after" with no discussion of what that really entails. Is that like suspended animation, or perhaps a kyrogenic freeze? Such is the life of a princess, right? Yeah, that is until the peasants rise up in revolt or an invading army marches in. Even the princess doesn't get to be suspended in perfect castle life forever. At least, it is unlikely.

There are places I thought I would live forever and furniture I thought I'd always have, but I have moved so many times in my adult life, and I've lost everything twice. The place I live now is the second longest residence of my adulthood, just over six years. It has been a struggle to keep it and stay housed, but I cannot fear the future, I have to say, come what may.

Fearing change is futile. We are creatures of change. This is a life of change, we change and we grow. Holding on physically or emotionally to people, places, and things we have outgrown, lost, or had torn from us holds us hostage to the past. The past is gone.

Change is life, and to embrace change despite the societal nonsense we have been taught will keep us thriving and moving forward. To hold the home, the partner, the job, as security when there is no security outside of ourselves. It is a trick of our own ego, and a trick of society to keep us locked into the status quo. Break free and accept change as part of the marvel on this spinning ball of blue!

WHAT iS A SUCCESSFUL RELATiONSHiP?

What is a Successful Relationship? Is it long, or short? Is it platonic or romantic, (can it be both)? Is it monogamous, or polyamorous? My understanding of a successful relationship has changed a lot over the last 5 years.

All relationships are unique. No two are the same. People bring out different aspects of our character and vice versa. People in our lives feed differing needs we have. Two people who bring out the worst in each other can bring out the best with another. Someone can be a lousy parent, but offer something else great into the world.

Relationships take compromise. But a successful relationship needs limits to that compromise. It can't be the same person doing all of the compromising, and we can't be doing things that compromise our personal values, at least not without a great deal of internal or relational conflict.

Good relationships are friendships. If you don't feel like your partner in life is your closest friend, why not? Are you taking each other for granted? Do you have resentments or water under the bridge you or they cannot get over? If so, that is no way to spend the final quarter of this life. If you need to talk, have an honest conversation. If you need counseling, try that. Try to get back to that original friendship you had in the beginning.

All relationships ebb and flow. The waves can pound the shore sometimes, and storms can be long, but then the sun comes out and the tide is again gentle and rolling. A successful relationship can weather a storm and build even stronger bonds because of it. Relationships can heal. However, if you are beating a dead horse and are together merely out of habit, perceived necessity, or fear of change, is that really how you want your last days to be?

I used to say my marriage was successful. I believed it was, it spanned more than two decades. But one day, poof! It was over and done. I always thought a long relationship was a success, but it's not if one or both are unfulfilled or miserable. It's not if it's cruel or vindictive on one side or both. It's not if you are walking on eggshells.

Since my own marriage ended in 2019, I've had talks with people who are in long term stagnant relationships, people who haven't been intimate in years, or sleep in separate rooms. If that works for you that's great, but those I have met feel emotionally alone and yet trapped in a burdensome legacy they feel compelled to stick with. But why? Because society says so, or your family, or who?

I can admit now that I never wanted to be divorced. I never wanted to have an "ex-husband". It sounded yucky; I still have a hard time saying it. I use all kinds of work arounds to avoid saying "ex-husband". Isn't that silly? My current favorite is borrowed from a neighbor: "when I was married...".

Please understand, it doesn't bother me at all if other people say "ex", or have an ex, but for me I did not want that. I always said that if I married it was for life, and I meant it. But in not wanting to be divorced I endured a lot of undeserved hardship and overbearing control. I was constantly minimized as a person and a partner. Was that really a success?

As crushed as I was by getting dumped, the realization of the strain I'd been living under was a shock! I spent 20 years being bullied and demeaned. I couldn't see how it was while I was in it. Suddenly no one was there belittling me for minor stuff like bumping the curb while parking. I realized, while relationships do indeed ebb and flow, (and in a decades-long relationship there can be a bad few months, even a bad year), sometimes we just get used to the hard times and never realize there could be something better for us. Yes, even at this age. Maybe even being alone is better than that?

Admittedly, my experience is extreme. I spent a lot of time accepting treatment I should not have accepted because I thought I was building a full life with someone. Not realizing that maybe I was accepting too much unacceptable behavior because of the commitment I made, probably also the fear of starting over, and a fear of what I believed could be an ugly breakup. After he left, I realized that I could have blindly stayed in that relationship until the end of my days.

In the five years since, I've had five romantic liaisons. Two were really good, two were spectacular disasters, and one was 50/50, but we're still friendly. One of the spectacular disasters is still a close friend. Whatever. Life is complex, and so are relationships.

A former lover told me, "I feel like with every relationship I get better and better". It struck me when he said it, and I have thought of those words often. What a beautiful statement. What a great way to think of our relationships! We are striving to be better and better -- any relationship old or new can benefit from that perspective.

Over these last years, I've learned a surprising lot about relationships from my friends who have never been married or have been married multiple times. Their embrace of change and willingness to experience heartbreak and still try it again is powerful in my eyes. Often they are still close friends with some of their former partners. People who are co-parenting successfully with a former partner, that is really impressive to me. I'm not sure I would have said that a decade ago.

Mutual respect, honor, honesty, loyalty: this is love, and it's what makes a successful relationship. If we lose that what is the point?

If you're in a partnership, give it some scrutiny. How could it be better? How can you make it better? Are there things you need to address with the other person?

If you're in a kind of lackluster situation with someone, what can you do to fix it? Can it be fixed? Sometimes in long relationships people grow apart, and sometimes we grow back together. I'll say it yet again, relationships ebb and flow, there are good times and bad, and sometimes the good times are so good we can get through the bad times easier. Sometimes the bad is so bad no good day can fix it.

If you're in a strong and loving partnership, good for you!! You've weathered the storms of life, and that's great! Congratulations! Honor that bond! Celebrate every day! If you are newly wed, or together less than five years, congratulations to you and your optimism! Building a life together is a wondrous thing, no doubt about it!

Maybe you're polyamorous, with evolving and committed partners. Life is change; good for you for accepting and embracing what you need. Lots of people think they want an open relationship or to be polyamorous, but their emotions get in the way, their lack of emotional intelligence and strong personal foundation makes it too hard. I bow to those who make it work.

Perhaps you prefer more casual relationships or "friends with benefits" as they say. There is nothing wrong with that. Different people need different things at different times in life. A casual relationship can be highly successful, or not. An intimate friendship can be a really beautiful thing. It doesn't matter how it looks or what others might say, what's right for you is just that!

Being alone too is right for some of us, it's what we need. Some people are asexual. We are all different with different needs and comfort levels. We are ever evolving, ever changing beings. Relationships are ever evolving too. Our original nature was to migrate with the seasons.

When I think about my relationship goals today, they are so different than when I was single before. And of course they would be! I'm not 25, my goals and dreams are completely different now. I am not looking for the same thing in a relationship today. I had to really think about what I was looking for. Maybe I am not looking for a life partner? I'm not sure.

I have grown so much in the last five years from the relationships and friendships I have cultivated and all I have experienced, and from time alone to create, to rest, and be with my thoughts. Right now it seems I need a lot of time alone. But also I have developed some amazing friendships over these years. I've had really tender and intimate experiences with lovers. I've been in two relationships spanning several years. They are serious friendships - committed, but not partners.

Nothing about my situation is typical, partly because my divorce took four long years - a year just to serve the papers! It seemed weird and unfair to be in any kind of serious relationship while going through the mess of that. Even now, I don't want to put anyone through bonus turmoil for being my friend.

In my healing journey, I have come far. Far enough to know what I can handle relationship-wise. Far enough to let love into my life with some of my best relationships ever, both platonic and romantic. Far enough to feel like my experiences and learning were important enough to share here in hope of helping others. But not far enough to trust that I could be in a healthy co-habitative relationship at this time. I could see myself losing the ground I've made. I need to learn that having a partnership doesn't come at the expense of what I need to do in my life or who I am. All that scares me a little, but it's why I go to therapy. I am always trying to figure myself out and do better. I don't want to stagnate in life or in relationships.

I guess I am speaking of our path in life again. Each of us has a path in life we are on, it is determined by us - our inherited genes, where the stars and planets were at our birth, and the personality we were born with. No two of us are on the same path. But our paths weave, and sometimes we share the path of another. However, we can only share a path with another for periods of time. In a healthy long relationship, each person is on their own path, but their paths sometimes match up for different things and periods of time. They separate for a while and then come back together. Not to say the time on those separate paths is necessarily bad or rocky, it can be seamless. But, it HAS to exist for the relationship to remain fulfilling for both parties.

An example might be a couple who is together for 15 years, and in that time they had two children and found a house in a small town they liked. In those instances of making and raising a family, and buying and maintaining their home, they are on the same path or on paths next to each other. Then one takes time to get a higher level of education, or one has strong career goals of their own. In those parts of their lives they are on their own path. Both are vital to a healthy partnership. If one partner just remains on the path of the other, problems arise. Then there is conflict, and how that plays out determines our future. It cannot be avoided.

No path can be a superhighway for all, they bump and weave. A successful relationship allows for unity and the autonomy of each partner and honors it.

Sounds so simple.

CONFLICT HAPPENS IN ALL RELATIONSHIPS

All relationships have conflicts, no relationship can grow without it. Conflict, when dealt with honestly and in good faith, can make a relationship stronger and better. It is also the place where the most toxic parts of relationships usually lurk. It's because few of us see it or learn good conflict resolution from our parents, because they were never taught it either.

Conflict requires kindness and negotiation. It is how we act and react in times of conflict that makes for a healthy relationship that can grow and improve from the conflict, or it cannot and the relationship ends, or it cannot yet people remain together while growing more and more apart.

Some conflicts are small, like the challenge of making plans when time is short. Some conflicts are big, maybe filled with some choice language. That stuff happens, but if it's always loud and angry there may lie a problem.

In my own marriage, we tried various things to keep arguments from escalating. We were often working to improve things and find better conflict resolution. One thing we started doing that helped a lot was going for a walk to discuss it if we started to have a misunderstanding. One or the other of us would say, "Put your shoes on, we're going...", sometimes through clenched teeth. More often than not, the walk improved our moods and resolved the problem. It was outside, so my husband had to watch his tone. We could take time to hear each other out. There was time and space for discussion over what was said, how it was interpreted, what was really meant, and so on. Miscommunications could be resolved. Not to mention birds chirping and wind in the trees, all of that certainly helped. After 20 minutes or half an hour, we would usually have it all sorted out.

The thing is, conflict is going to exist in any relationship, with every one we know, at some point, at some level. With friends, family, lovers, and co-workers, conflicts are going to arise. It's how we deal with conflict which makes all the difference. Losing our tempers happens to everyone, but let's admit it's child behavior. It looks good on nobody. Most of all, things said in anger cannot be unsaid. Big showy drama scenes and overreaction are awful to come back from, and things can become irreparable.

Some people attempt to ignore or otherwise not address conflicts when they arise, as if it will go away in the silence of it. This is never a good idea in an honest relationship. The silence becomes a hematoma taking blood from every healthy part of the relationship until it is all anemic.

That's where friendship comes in, and honest communication. Sometimes bridges come down, sometimes they just need repair, all relationships require preventative maintenance. Dealing with conflict in an honest, loving way can make a relationship stronger than ever. Face it, address it, resolve it, and move on from it. Ha! Did I just accidentally create a new acronym? F.A.R.M. your conflict! There we go!

Dwelling on mistakes, ours or others, creating a relationship tally sheet, that is no way to live. Watch some videos, read some articles on how to argue in a healthy way. You will probably be surprised that both sides are usually guilty of some negative behavior or bad conflict habits that could be improved or resolved with a little effort. We are all in this together.

All of humankind is full of foibles and quirks. When I was around 16, I proclaimed, "Everyone is crazy, it's a matter of finding people whose neurosis you can deal with!"

A Brief On Friendship

Here I was, 52 years old and pondering what a friend truly is. What makes a person a friend? Such a seemingly simple thing became a huge epiphany for me to finally understand friendship, and how being or having a friend can be simply measured. I've written about it more for another project, but I'll briefly share it here. I'm glad to share it anywhere! It has been a big help in understanding so much of my life. It became a simple measure I could put any relationship up to, past or present, to know if someone was a friend or not.

My measure is this, the base level of friendship is being a "well wisher". This means someone who wishes the best for you. They wish you success and good fortune with no tie to it except that they like you. That's how I feel about all of my friends and many more beyond. I wish pretty much everyone I encounter well, but I am extreme. I also say hello to everyone on the street. Many others are more discerning on that front. Friendship certainly has levels.

How does one define that warm feeling inside of us in the presence of certain others, that rosiness we shine onto them and they us? That's well-wishing, plain and simple.

Every friendship is different; there are levels, and there is give and take.

Who do you call when you have a flat tire? I would have said AAA, but today I do have a handful of friends I can count on in an emergency, and they can count on me. At least I try my best. Sometimes we let one another down, but as long as we remember we are all well-wishers, no one's feelings are hurt. With this understanding, friendship can become pretty carefree and beautiful. We won't feel crushed when our friends sometimes let us down. If there is cause for concern, it is addressed.

If I don't wish you well, I just don't want to be around you. I'm never going to tear someone down, or wish them poorly behind their back or in my head. No thanks! I have no time for such nonsense. Honestly, I wish most people well. If I don't wish someone well it's rare, and they have likely wronged me or are part of something I am vehemently against.

I might have a candid conversation with a friend if I am concerned about their well being. I might get frustrated with them. But that is part of well wishing. Sometimes it sucks when we want the best for our friends and those we love, but they don't want that for themselves.

It's no joke, we are all going through a lot of stuff. We are all looking through different colored glasses, and maybe there's a war inside our head (to paraphrase a Suicidal Tendencies song). If we are let down by a friend, we should re-evaluate. Was it malicious? Or was it just they couldn't assist in that moment? We shouldn't be crushed either way.

I have learned if someone is telling me who they are, I need to listen. When someone in my life is acting with malice, in bad faith, or sadistic intent, it is usually evident. They give all kinds of hints and signs. They are people who cross boundaries, or act disrespectfully. In the past I might have tried to win them over like a feral cat we want to tame, but today I step away.

Now armed with a measure, we can observe the people in our lives and see easily who actually wishes us well. However, it can also be a painful realization to see those in our lives who are not well-wishers. It is rough when some of our closest attachments are actually frenemies, or worse.

Friendship is also give and take; you give what you can and you take what you need. What you can give is different than giving all you have, and it is different in every relationship. Taking what you need is also vital. Friends feed different parts of our being and we them. If you don't want anything from the friendship, then do you have an ulterior motive? We all want and need things from our friends. It may simply be quiet companionship, respect, and love. I used to think asking for help was wrong and I had to do it all myself, but now I accept that I need other people. We all want to give, and we all have needs when it comes to the people in our lives.

We are closer to some friends than others, but it doesn't make them less or more well wishers. Just as some friends have come and gone, swept away in the tidal changes of life. More friends we don't yet know will someday come into our lives. I have friends I see at 10 or 20 year intervals and we are still right there, synced, like no time has passed.

Today, I have a small circle of close friends, and a larger circle of faraway friends and friendly acquaintances. I've learned that just showing up is a big part of friendship. You don't need to be flashy or rich, or the life of the party, just being a well wisher is enough. As a well wisher, I approach friendship with honor and reverence for another.

My friends are a strange and beautiful brood. They are from every walk of life, and we are all perfectly imperfect. I don't need to surround myself with oranges if I am an orange, I can share camaraderie with apples, bananas, fish, trees, and even Brussels sprouts.

FRENEMIES

We've probably all been on both sides of this at some point in our lifetime. I can only speak for myself, but typically any time I have been around someone who I did not wish the best for, I chose not to be around them. If I don't like someone, it's probably for a good reason. I don't care what kind of title you hold. Can I forgive? Sure. I forgive for my own well-being and good health. Do I still want to hang out? No thanks. There are probably ten million people on this planet who could and would be my friend, so I'll just keep seeking them out. I like pretty much everyone until they give me a reason not to. By keeping things simple I avoid a lot of problems.

I have been envious of friends a few times. I have coveted some accomplishments, or maybe started to look over in a "grass is always greener" way. But if I am honest, those reactions always came from me not being happy with my own self and my own accomplishments or lack thereof. It was really about me not feeling good about myself, or not being able to express myself like I wanted. In the end, it was about me, not them.

If you are a person who gets upset when your friend has success or you get jealous of another's life, relationship, or achievements, that is about you, not them. Once I decided to start living like I wanted to live, doing the things I wanted to do, and stretching to seek and learn and grow, once I did that, I have never felt envious of another again. I am joyful for my friends when good things are happening for them. I'm not angry at someone's success. I know we are all on our own path. I also believe "a high tide raises all boats" and I am all for that!

For me, I don't like the way not liking someone makes me feel, so I avoid people i don't like, or I seek out something to like about them. Not even to say they are bad people necessarily; maybe our magnetics are off in some way. But I trust my gut if someone repels me. I like most people, I believe people are good, and I have friends from a wide walk of lives. I don't need to agree with you to be your friend. No two people can agree on everything. If someone proves themself a frenemy or a full blown enemy, I am going to walk away and stay away. I don't enjoy intrigues or drama or betrayal, and I don't need to accept it.

If you find yourself angry or upset at your friends' successes, then maybe you need to ask a different question...

DO YOU LOVE YOURSELF?

Your first and best friendship has got to be your relationship with yourself. How many of us have reached this age with self loathing or an angry inner voice? Stop having a bad relationship with yourself and you will stop having bad relationships with others.

Only if you love yourself can you truly love another. That phrase used to really irritate me, and then I realized that when people don't love themselves they need people for all the wrong reasons. You don't have the capacity because you are dealing with a deficit of some sort. You must have some level of self love, self trust, and self care in order to have something to share with another.

If you don't love yourself, you'll spend your life trying to get validation from others and that is a bad way to go. Our first responsibility is to ourselves. For women especially, we are taught to sacrifice, that it is noble to put our dreams aside to care for our families, partners, children, and parents. We spend so much of our time trying to get approval from others, we miss living. I never felt I measured up. I was always trying to overcompensate by working too hard, or putting others ahead of me who would not do the same. Some people took advantage of that, but only a few. I didn't see it for a long time because I had a low opinion of myself.

Today I feel free of that kind of scrutiny from outside myself, and from my inside too. I do the best I can every day to honor this life and this vessel. Over are the days of harsh self-criticism, and it took a long time to shake all that.

One of the things I did right after my husband left, (barely a week into it, in fact) was drive over to Microcosm Books on my lunch hour from work and get a couple zines. I was still in shock and acting automatically, but what a gift I gave to myself! They do a "5-Minute Therapy" zine series with Dr. Faith Harper. One called "Self Compassion" changed my life. In it she asks the question, (and I'm paraphrasing here, something like) "If your inner critic, was a real person and they were talking to someone you care about the way they talk to you, what would you say about that relationship?"

That really caught me. My inner critic had become so cruel, it acted like a mean prison guard. I spent months afterward consciously trying to retrain my inner voice to be kinder and less critical. Why was I so angry at myself inside? What a bizarre thing that we have an enemy inside us. Why would our inner voice be anything less than encouraging?

I started using guided meditations off YouTube, I used psychedelics, and I took long nature walks with my dear fur-son, Lucy. I went to therapy and prioritized improving my relationship with myself.

One thing I did, and continue to do, is if I passed a mirror, I made a point to look into my eyes and smile at myself. I don't know if I read this somewhere or if I just came up with it on my own, but it seems to help. For example, when I use the bathroom, I do it while I'm washing my hands. I know that sounds silly, but it has helped me a ton. I always used to say, "I gotta be able to look at myself in the mirror", meaning I always want to be an honorable person in all matters. That comes from my parents, I suppose. Then, one day, I thought about how looking in the mirror could also be about reassuring myself, so I decided giving myself an encouraging smile was important for being my own best friend. One of my silly experiments, but it worked. I thought if someone smiling at me made me feel better, certainly my own reassuring smile would too. I suppose this is probably an inner child healing practice of some sort. A reassurance practice.

What is a good life? I would guess it's similar for most people: a good sense of self, many moments of joy, a life of pursuing one's own dreams and goals. It's not too late for any of that. In fact, if we follow the orca's lead we are right on time! But part of being able to lead is knowing and trusting ourselves, being self-reliant, and following our intuition. We can't do any of that if we are full of self-doubt and letting ourselves down.

Learning self-compassion and self-love is vitally important. Tame your inner critic, and reach out to your inner child. Learn healthy ways to cope with the emotions of stress and reactions to life's hurdles. Learn to communicate your feelings in positive, direct, and honest ways. Spend time alone, meditate, ask yourself questions, learn to know yourself and appreciate your strengths and weaknesses.

I've been pretty honest that I used hallucinogens including psilocybin mushrooms in small doses, to process the grief of the death of my marriage. I also used them during meditations to heal my inner child and reach higher consciousness. I'm not ashamed of that. I understand that might not be for everyone. So little is known about the power of the mind and what it is capable of, both on its own and with help from some magical mushrooms, or ketamine, or DMT, or whatever you prefer, or nothing at all. I am introspective and I want to get better all the time. I want to live this life fully and totally. I want to stand up for what I believe, and say what I think, and live as I wish. I will love as I dare, freely and openly now and forever. Whatever that looks like might not be conventional. It is not conventional, and I doubt it ever will be.

Welcome yourself home to you. You deserve to be loved by the most important person in your life, your self. We are often far too hard on ourselves, harder than we would ever be to anyone else. Stop abusing yourself, stop selling yourself short, stop the criticism that is not constructive.

Think of all you have done and how hard you have tried, and give yourself a pat on the back for all that, a smile in the mirror, a little present. You deserve it. And, if you really feel you don't deserve good things, maybe try harder to be the person that you believe does deserve good things. We can all improve.

SHADOW SiDE WORKOUT: FOR A FUTURE WiTHOUT CHAiNS

It's time to work out your dark side. That means identifying the things that are holding you back from being all you want to be. Let go of that faulty early imprinting that keeps you feeling bad about yourself, and maybe hurting yourself with coping mechanisms that used to work. Maybe they don't work so good after all? Let's free ourselves from that bondage once and for all, so we can go to our graves knowing true freedom and joy, and unshackled from our past.

Seldom is it that any of us reach adulthood unscathed from trauma or without some unhealthy thinking pattern, emotional vulnerability, or coping mechanism. Personally, I have some pretty intense PTSD I've been working through. I bite my nails, I have nervous stomach so bad I sometimes poo blood, and somewhere down the road of life I got the idea that I was in debt to others?!?! None of us are just one thing. All of us are light and dark, good and bad. I was also a strong, independent woman who time and again proved I could do anything I set my mind to. Except I could not seem to appreciate my own achievements at all.

There is service, and there is servile. We all owe it to our fellow man to serve each other, to act in brotherhood and sisterhood to our neighbors, but not in a way that is detrimental to our own being. Instead of being in service, I was in servitude. I had developed some weird behaviors that kept me always putting those around me first in a way that harmed my own goals and self-hood. This weird over-obligation to others was sometimes self-destructive, or at least self-hindering. It kept me from striving. It kept me feeling small and insignificant - even to myself.

In 'The War Of Art' Steven Pressfield would call that "resistance". Indeed, it was a great way to hide fear. Fear of failure, fear of success, fear of being judged, not sure which. All of it, I guess? But I could not see it. I guess that is what makes it "Shadow Work" or makes addressing our darker side so difficult. It can hide in seemingly normal thoughts and actions.

The phrase "Shadow Work" sounds like some Dorian Grey existential crisis, doesn't it? Don't look at the painting in the attic!!! Seriously though, I think of it as the shadow we cast rather than some dark skeletons in the closet. We all cast a shadow in the sun. The less desirable traits of our personality don't have to be some secret heroin habit, or a string of motel sex encounters. For me it was simply over-obligating myself, squelching my goals and dreams for those of others, and a general lack of boundaries. Over the last three or four years, I have faced many of these issues either emotionally, or in life, or both. I have searched out where these feelings have been hidden and coded into my actions. Letting go of those things has helped me so much. I have never felt so free and unburdened. Crazy that it took until my fifties to get here, but I'll take it.

HAPPiNESS iS AN iNSiDE JOB

My mother always told me "Happiness is an inside job". I may even say it elsewhere within these pages.

To me, this means nothing outside of us can make us happy; we can only find true happiness from ourselves. We control if we are happy or sad. If someone is making us feel anything, that is actually us allowing ourselves to feel a certain way. Sharing our happiness in a relationship, a career, or a pursuit is more accurate than deriving happiness FROM those things.

This concept has served me well in life. It has allowed me to face change, challenge, or misfortune optimistically. It has allowed me to find creative outlets to still experience happiness in times of struggle. Studio time is never more important to the artist than when they are struggling elsewhere in life. We all must enjoy the pursuit of happiness.

I've had bad times, but I'd never say I had it bad. I've had it pretty good in life. I have been happy most of my life. No matter how bad things might get, I always had myself. I could find joy just walking the dog, and I walked the dog a lot. I've been lucky to have wonderful canine companions over the years!

I took "Happiness is an inside job" as truth and worked hard to maintain a cheery disposition no matter what was happening around me. This is a really great outlook, but it also gave me a feeling of guilt if I ever felt anything except happy. Another unfortunate side effect meant some people close to me could do lousy stuff. Stuff that should not have been overlooked, but because happiness was an inside job, I couldn't let it bother me - even though there are things that really should have bothered me! It became sometimes a kind of Pollyanna existence.

No one is going to be happy a hundred percent of the time, and to expect to be, or be expected to be, can only go on for so long. Also, people need to be held accountable when they wrong us. Sure, forgive, that is for our own well-being. But to overlook trespasses and let them happen again and again, because "Happiness is an inside job" is wrong. This is something I had a hard time learning.

While I felt responsible for my own happiness, I also felt responsible for certain other people's happiness. Somehow I dismissed the point that it is up to each of us to supply for ourselves. We cannot create happiness for another no matter how badly we wish to. It is a personal choice, and unhappiness is too. I'm not suggesting depression is not real, but at some point, if we can't bring it for ourselves, no one and nothing else can bring happiness to us. It must come from and reside within us. Happiness is an inside job for each of us - we must live in the pursuit of happiness for ourselves.

When someone is constantly trying to bring us down, acting out, or spreading misery, we cannot just keep brushing it off. It will affect us at some point. We are trading molecules all the time, therefore we must be cautious who we are close to. It's sad and difficult to accept that sometimes a toxic person just needs to be cut from our lives, especially if they have an important title like parent, sibling or spouse.

BACK TO THAT DEBT THING

If someone had told me that many of the problems holding me back were from a sense of debt, or a required martyrdom of myself for others, I would have scoffed at them. But it was true, and when the understanding finally came, I realized it began with compartmentalizing the things I could not cope with, a coping mechanism from childhood apparently. I hid moments from myself, mostly centered around betrayals or malice at the hands of others. I shrugged off back stabs like someone else might shrug off a less than great meal at their favorite restaurant. My resiliency was astonishing, but why was I allowing people to harm me?

It took until my early 50s, after the end of my sometimes beautiful, sometimes ugly marriage, and because someone I had come to regard as a close friend had betrayed me. Oddly enough, the ordeal ended up being one of the best things that ever happened to me!

Allow me to say here, this is embarrassing to admit. I don't want to admit a weakness like this to the public. I'm not looking for any congratulations. I share it because I did not even realize I had this feeling until age 52. If I have shit I am holding onto that is this absurd, there is a good likelihood you have something too - something that has created anger, or longing, or some hardship, and it's probably from something that happened in your childhood.

When I was first seeing a trauma therapist, she spoke of using a process called EMDR (Eye Movement Desensitization and Reprocessing) to process traumatic events in our life. My therapist explained that we usually process traumatic experiences in our sleep, but sometimes something is skipped for whatever reason and that is where we develop trauma and/or PTSD. When we discussed what would be an event to use EMDR for, she said these were the memories that did not fade like old photos, they remained clear and bright every single time you recalled them. Thinking on it for a few weeks, the episodes I was identifying were kind of surprising events that maybe I had not thought much about, or were not traditional trauma. The big traumas in my life, like violence or rape had been pretty well resolved. We all have something. I'm not saying we all compartmentalize anger or hurt we don't feel we can address, that was my issue. But maybe there is something inside you causing you pain, causing you to have less than the life you want in some way?

I'm realizing now, when people hurt me, I reacted by believing I was to blame, so rather than righteous anger I often reacted with guilt. As though my hurt feelings was a mark against me and meant I was bad, rather than the person who'd mistreated me in some way. It sounds ridiculous when I write it here, but I am on the other side of it now. I can see clearly how those absurd beliefs allowed me to have no boundaries. I learned we can't have boundaries if somewhere in our subconscious we have come to believe we do not deserve them.

I'm still learning and growing from this. It's a struggle every day, but I am excited to have these freedoms grow within me and these epiphanies bloom, no matter how hard.

Compartmentalizing, or "stuffing" as I called it, was me essentially hiding things from myself, such as how mean someone was being, or in instances of betrayal. I stuffed it, especially if the betrayer was a loved one. Sure, that worked, but it was no way to live. The more recent episode with my close friend made me see I was hiding their other instances of betrayal, gaslighting, and dishonesty from myself, but I guess my compartments were all full! I realized I was having memory issues not unlike early dementia. I was terrified. It sent me on a downward spiral of sorrow, fear, inadequacy, and so forth. I felt like I was falling apart mentally. It went on for weeks, maybe longer.

The resolution of it all came via a dark night of the soul, using meditation (one guided meditation in particular), a hot bath, and a fair dose of mushrooms. It sent me flying through my mind and walking backward in my own life until I realized where in my youth the practice had begun. When I was able to look at it with healthy, safe, adult eyes, I could see how compartmentalizing this one thing that I should not have affected my entire life.

Through the process - a hell ride that felt like eternity, but was more like a few hours - all of the compartments opened and a lifetime of experiences I'd hidden from myself floated out of the multitude of drawers inside me, rolling over me, and into the ether. As I emerged from this dark night of the soul, I felt so different, so light, so free. No more fog, no more forgetfulness. I scrolled through one of my social media profiles and saw myself in photos for maybe the first time. It turns out I was not a hideous monster like I thought I was, I was actually pretty! All these years I had no idea.

This debt showed itself in lack of boundaries, but also in a self-sabotage that was spurred from not wanting to outshine anyone. Outshining some people, even potentially or perceptionally, had resulted in me being harmed in different ways, so as long as I stayed in the background everything was cool. But why would a person live like that?

I guess we get brainwashed? At least I did. Like a Stockholm Syndrome of some sort. I finally realized I was being held hostage, by myself for others. In Stockholm Syndrome, essentially one acquiesces a little, and then a little more, and soon our boundaries are so low we can't even limbo under the stick. The sad and terrible case of Colleen Stan's kidnapping, and spending nearly a decade living in a box under the bed of her kidnappers, ought to illustrate to the world the extreme version of what happens when young women do not have a strong sense of themselves. In America, that is most women.

"Good Fences Make Good Neighbors", that was something my father used to say. It's a good metaphor in this instance. If our boundaries are firm and healthy, we can be a great neighbor. If not, we open our home up to riffraff or squatters, and/or it ends up in disrepair because we aren't for ourselves. We are letting the squatters and riffraff break and steal our treasures, such as our self-esteem.

FUCK FRENEMIES, ALL WOMEN ARE SISTERS

I know I have spoken about frenemies elsewhere, but I want to say here, we need to embrace our sisterhood. I will be the first to admit that most of my closest friends in life have been male. I don't hate my sisters, but I have been burned enough times to be leery.

In recent years, I have chosen to let down my guard completely with other women. Now that have boundaries like a person is supposed to, I have little fear these days of getting into a position to be burned by a friend. Sure, there are some damaged people out there, but I am no longer attracting that kind of energy into my life. I have learned to say no. Nor do I feel any jealousy or envy. I'm not comparing myself to anyone. I am not in a race.

I am really happy over here in Amy-land, and if you want to celebrate with me, come on down! If you want to beat me down, I might try to help you see things differently, but I'm also gonna get out of harm's way. I will never deny my instincts or gut intuition again. Self-preservation is the highest law, and if someone is looking at me with envy, or malice, or is giving off a vibe that they don't like themselves, I will step away. Walking this earth with others can be in cooperation or competition. I prefer to cooperate and raise each other up, I want to live in that world. I will no longer accept anything less.

IT'S TIME TO WORK OUT YOUR DARK SIDE

Years ago, the great artist and my dear friend Dave Archer wisely warned that somewhere around our late forties, all life's traumas that haven't been dealt with will come to out to play, and you have to face them or die. Before Dave was a world renowned painter, he spent his early adult life working in San Francisco as a doorman and a hustler. I loved his stories of adventures, like hanging with Janis Joplin when she was playing coffee shops for hamburgers. He said they both came to San Francisco because they worshiped the Beats, but the Beats were gone when they got there. He was most famous for painting images of outer space with a Tesla coil. He used a million volt Tesla coil to reverse paint on glass. His paintings of the most amazing galaxies and planets rivaled the views from the Hubble telescope. He was literally hitting paint with a lightning bolt to create magic! He became world famous, appearing on 'Ripley's Believe It Or Not' in comic strips and on the TV show. Working with 'Star Trek: The Next Generation' he made all the art on the walls of The Enterprise. He did so much! Forgive me, I could go on and on, and tell so many stories of the magician, artist, and scholar Dave Archer! But back to his warning about our hidden traumas, fears, insecurities, and self-sabotage, which we all have suffered in one form or another. We need to work them out now if we haven't already. Those words have proven very true for me, and I've seen others, peers unwilling or unable to cope with or resolve their issues at this stage in life, much to their detriment.

We need to look at these things, and uncover their origins. It's hard and it's ugly. But you don't want to die dragging those chains to your grave. I've come to face quite a few of my demons these last few years. Mine are mostly feelings of inadequacy that I'd carried around from some faulty beliefs. It's embarrassing to admit but identifying and resolving this changed my life so much. For too long, I approached every relationship, whether work, romance, or friends, as though I was in debt to the other person. It caused me to act slavishly at jobs, and in some of my relationships. It made me want to prove myself, which sounds really good, but it didn't always serve me. I put my own goals and projects aside too much to assist others with what I perceived as their more important things.

The fact that I approached all relationships like debts was totally subconscious. I had no idea I felt like a bad person for being betrayed. That is just bizarre! Letting go of that freed me like nothing else. It was a hell ride. I barely survived, but today I am a changed person. Safe boundaries were instantly erected, fears let go of, and as I said, I think I saw myself for the first time ever.

Now I know, I am enough. I don't owe anyone anything for being me. If you like me, here I am. If you don't, then "see ya". I'm not going to try to win anyone over. I don't care. If you don't like me, cool, let's not hang out. I'm not keen on the whole "frenemy" scene. No thanks.

LEARNING OUR BOUNDARIES

If someone is crossing a boundary with me today, I simply let them know. Or I ask them "What's wrong?" But, it took a long time to get here. I have also realized in more recent incidents of deception or betrayal that the person was acting based on issues they had, and it really was all about them. Maybe they don't love themselves as much as they should?

People tell themselves acting in an underhanded way, or with ulterior motives, is just how the world works. Not my world. I try to be an honorable person in all of my actions, and now I try to surround myself with others who feel the same. Today, I'm honest about what doesn't work for me. If I identify some troubling behavior with another, I'll address it or simply step away from the situation. Of course everyone has bad days and hard times, and I welcome friends to lean on me, but no one is gonna guilt me into anything. Also, if someone is constantly being negative, I can accept I have to stay away, or at least limit access for my own well-being.

I have never felt freer, as painful as peering into my dark side was, it was worth everything to no longer compartmentalize bad things that happen. I don't need to hide anything from myself anymore. Today, I have a clear understanding of my boundaries. I'm not going to wait to get mad about it, or allow myself to be hurt or harmed in some way. I don't even feel like I need to "be vigilant" about keeping up my boundaries. They are solid in their foundation. I am honest and clear if someone crosses a line with me, before it becomes a problem.

I can say no. I don't have feelings to over-give or over-prove myself. Sometimes I get a bit of a "ghost feeling" for it, like a ghost limb, but I can identify it and talk myself down. I'm okay with being me, I am good enough, and now that I realize that, I have such a sense of ease. Things are much better in my life and in all of my relationships.

If we are truly going to be a friend to ourself, we need to ask ourself "What issues aren't we dealing with?" It hurts, it's embarrassing, but I am so thankful I went deep and resolved some of this stuff.

GENERATIONAL TRAUMA

When my mother died a few years ago, I did me a little ritual to burn away and free myself and all those in my line from our generational trauma. It was so effective that at first I felt as though I had given my whole self away, that I'd burned up all of who I was because I guess I was built on so much generational trauma, probably most of us are.

I burned my generational trauma in the form of a partially burned sage smudge that I'd had for several years on my alter. I probably should have waited, but I did it three days after my mother's death.

I sat outside and started a small fire in my backyard. When the fire began to burn steady, I focused all my thoughts of generational trauma on the sage smudge. The smudge had come from an international night market a few blocks from my house. I bought it from three young women selling witchy wares at a table. It was a really large and dense twist of sage. I had burned a bit of it once or twice to clear the house up after a departure or two, as one might imagine. But it was far too big a smudge for cleansing a house, I figured it could cleanse the trauma of my entire family line, outside under the stars.

I burned it for all of us, for the benefit of my mother's spirit and my father's spirit too. And their parents and grandparents. For all of us, for all my family to be free, to go forth free without those chains and shackles. It felt powerful, it was certainly powerful for me.

It hurt like hell. I was also shocked by how much of it was who I was. As it was going up in smoke, I realized how much of who I was was going away with it. Suddenly, I wanted it back. I began to panic. It was too great a loss: my beautiful mum, and all of our shared suffering, passed generation on top of generation, through famines and illnesses, and every kind of smite; all the way back to the subjugation and slaughter of my pagan ancestors, forced to die or serve the gold thirsty Christians of yore. But let us not get into that. That seemingly tiny act of focusing all of my generational trauma on that over-sized sage smudge and burning it up made me realize how real our generational trauma and suffering is, and how it weighs upon us.

My parents were good-hearted people, but they were flawed human beings. They had insecurities and oppression that were passed to them, they passed to my sister and me. Not mental illness, but a lack of self-belief. A mentality of lack from a long line of lack. My father lived in housing projects for most of his childhood. His mother was married five times, the first time at 16. Her mother had come from Sweden with only a small chest of belongings. Who knows what she had left behind, what she lived through on the voyage, or what she experienced in America, but she killed herself when my father's mother was 12. I didn't know this terrible fact until recently. She was just a photo in a frame. I'd mentioned to my sister that I'd hung the photo our father said was his mother's mother from Sweden. That's when my sister shared the story of her sad departure and grandma's strife. It actually explained a lot about my father's mother who was always cold and sharp tongued. I felt sorry for disliking her as a kid. No wonder she was gruff.

My mother's family carried it's own tragedies. Her parents, while kind and gentle, struggled and lived mostly in poverty. Both died at only age 57. There was a lot of sorrow and suffering and pain coming down those lines. Sadness and oppression pumped in our veins. My parents struggled, but life was about more than money to them. Things could have been so different, if we started from a different place, a place of joy, and abundance and enough.

EXPERiENTiAL TRAUMA

At this point in life, there's no way we haven't taken some hearty blows. We've lost loved ones - some to accidents or crimes, others watching them fade slowly away. We've been dealt some cards. Maybe you've been divorced, maybe more than once. Most likely you have changed careers, or had a series of jobs in life. Maybe you lost everything. I have, twice. By now, most of us have survived terrible accidents or disasters, and so much more.

In his encouraging recording "The Strangest Secret" from the 1950s, which I listen to on the regular, Earl Nightingale speaks of life needing to be like a ship: sound, with a captain at the helm, a plan, navigation mapped, and weather tracked. I agree, but sometimes a storm just comes out of nowhere. If you've made it to menopause, you have certainly weathered some storms! Even those with a seemingly perfect life experience grief, loss, and sorrow.

My own life has held so many twists and turns, blind corners, and every manner of nonsense. I've moved some 20 times in my adult life. Both my parents are gone. I have a contentious divorce finally wrapping up, 4 years later and not well resolved... But fuck it all, I made it!!

Every morning when I wake up and every night when I go to bed, I thank the day, the world, the universe, my little home, all the trees and everyone around me. I wish the best for all my kin, all my kindred spirits, everyone and every creature, plant, insect, rock, drop of water. I share love with what I call "The Great Is All". I send love waves out of my heart to it, to all, to everything, to you. If we all sent love out every night from our beds before we fell asleep and again when we woke up, and in all of our actions throughout the day, imagine how the world could be forever changed. I know that sounds like hippie bullshit, but it seems science is proving what mythology has told us forever, and every enlightened being whose words we read, whether credited to Buddha or Jesus or the alien, all say one thing, love each other.

Years ago, I wrote brief bios on a handful of serial killers for a website dedicated to such things. I focused on killers all hailing from the Calumet

Region where I grew up. It's an industrial wasteland that runs along the southeast side of Chicago and into Indiana. In every instance, the person in question came from a twisted and/or unloving family situation, with some kind of incest involved. There was abuse. Love was withheld. Conditions in the home were horrible. Every single one. Things like molesting kids really fucks them up.

Did you know incest is exclusively a western issue? Tribal cultures don't have such perversions. If you are gonna point one out to me, then you probably already know they are the exception to the rule. Generally, no tribal cultures have or had incest. They had homosexuality, they had natural variations of masculine and feminine in their peoples certainly, but they just don't have incest. Interesting, huh?

It happens where people are corrupted by the western world. It's not a natural action of man, it's a mutation. What in our culture could cause it? Pollution? That seems like a realistic connection. Years ago when gas switched from leaded to unleaded, crime went down all over the country, especially in the inner cities where the gas fumes were more concentrated.

Organized religion is also to blame for incest. In desperation for some narrow minded elitism, so many have suffered. Christianity has been used to control and destroy for more than two thousand years. In recent history "followers" are filled with judgmental spite, fully opposite the love the man they claim to worship was said to speak about. He was about love, they say, but so many who follow are filled with hate. It always seems corruption and perversion run rampant together.

Allow me to say here: there are many Christians who follow the teachings of Christ truly and try to live as he did. These people are wonderful and lovely, and I count many of them among my friends. I'm not speaking of them. This is about dark ages stuff, gross and dirty, used to create suffering, now melded into society in disturbing ways. It's an attack on the body, but even more the psyche. Incest and rape are about power - primarily taking power away, it has little to do with sex. Sadly, it's bad all over, or so I hear, in many parts of the world, women cannot go out unescorted for fear of being assaulted. Yet we are half of the population!

Incest is kind of both generational and experiential trauma here. There's also any number of other traumas we endure, especially women, such as rape and domestic violence. I've experienced both. Other traumas could be being shot or stabbed in a crime, being in a terrible accident or witnessing a violent crime or terrible accident, being in war, other forms of child abuse, and so much more. If these are things you experienced, are you living in reaction to them? How are they affecting your life and relationships? Do you even know?

I mentioned before the EMDR treatment I received. I was given three treatments during the course of a year. It helped change my life in profound ways. I couldn't have gotten here without it. I am so thankful! I've talked to a few friends who have had EMDR, but did not experience the strong results I had, I feel really lucky for the esteemed practitioner I found.

The most measurable proof of my EMDR success was being able to fly in a plane without terror and dry heaves. In 2001, I was on a plane bound for Chicago from Austin, with a stop in Kansas City. At first everything was fine, but then we encountered a storm. The turbulence was terrible, but seasoned travelers across the aisle assured me this happened all the time, no big deal. They suspended any drink service and the flight attendants strapped in. We were dropping what felt like thousands of feet and tossing to and fro. Buckled in, my head smashing on the ceiling above. Not just me, everyone. I finally looked toward the flight attendants for some reassurance, but they were holding hands and crying. Numerous people around me were reciting the 23rd Psalm (I only knew it from the Venom song, 'Welcome to Hell'): "As I walk through the valley in the shadow of death, I shall fear no evil…. ".

It was a bad deal, and I thought we were goners. I puked my guts out in a handy airplane sickness bag or three. We landed in Kansas City and sat on the tarmac for several hours, unable to de-board. After that, the easygoing days of flying were gone. Now, when I flew, I puked and had panic attacks. I just wanted to jump out, no, claw my way out. I flew maybe three times since, in emergencies, but swore never again. Then in a single experience, EMDR resolved my fears and withheld the terror that coursed through my veins anytime I had to, or even merely contemplated, getting on a plane. After the treatment, (which seemed like not much, almost absurd), Lark, my therapist said, "You'll see, you'll be fine. You'll be eating snacks on the ride." Saying that, she suddenly looked serious. "Be sure to buy snacks for the flight, they don't really serve food anymore on planes."

I snickered at the preposterous idea of snacking on a plane… Yeah, sure I will.

However, there I was a few days later enjoying a sandwich, yogurt, and a Little Debbie snack cake, all while flying high and looking out the window over some fracked up mountain in New Mexico or Utah. It was crazy. I laughed out loud to myself a few times on the plane! Such a folly. How was I fine? No crunched up neck. No screaming fear. No worry at all, aside from my internal Greta Thunberg complaining about my carbon footprint. How could this be? Thirty minutes of EMDR, basically watching a giant q-tip wave back and forth, ended decades of misery and terror on planes. I was flabbergasted.

My story aside, what I am saying is this is the final quarter of your life - what haven't you dealt with inside that is still causing you pain? What is still tripping you up? What would you like to do better? Is some trick of the ego messing with you? What relationships do you want to resolve?

HEALiNG AND CARiNG FOR OUR iNNER CHiLD

I always kind of scoffed about the "inner child", but it is true that we learned some weird wrong stuff from things we saw, or misinterpreted, or strange scenarios interpreted correctly that we should not have been witnessing. My own inner child had some weird ideas. I started doing some short inner child guided meditations to work through the emotional struggles of preparing for my first solo art show in 2021. Those were more for encouraging my inner child to express itself. Later, in order to finish this project, I had to go deeper and see why I held myself back so often in life. I could be so courageous sometimes and so afraid others. Why? I began to meditate more on the subject, and I started to learn interesting stuff about myself.

I realized I feared outshining people around me, I often held back if I felt something I might do or say could be perceived as outdoing anyone around me. And because of that, in some of my adult relationships I took the back seat, even when I was really driving the car.

When I really tried to think of where it came from, one thing that came up was something that happened in elementary school. As I recall this story, it's funny the weird things that mark us in life. This experience centers around a second grade science assignment. I'd completely forgotten about this entire experience until meditating on this issue...

Mrs. Gruba, our science teacher, gave us an assignment due some weeks later, I cannot recall the timeline. We were to clip science related articles out of newspapers or magazines, or photocopy them at the library, as there was no Internet or computers in the 1970s. She said she expected three to five articles from each of us.

My parents were newshounds, and spent several hours every morning drinking coffee and reading two, or usually three newspapers. My father would go pick up the Chicago Tribune and the Chicago Sun-Times. The local newspaper The Hammond Times usually came to the door every morning via the paperboy who lived on the next block. Their coffee was made on the stove in a percolator. They only switched to a coffee maker in the late 1980s. Even at my young age of maybe eight, I enjoyed listening to my parents' banter discussing the various world issues and how each paper reported it and their own thoughts. It was endlessly fascinating.

One Chicago paper leaned left, the other right. My parents felt they could piece the truth together by reading both. The local paper, "The Hammond Fish-wrapper" as my father sarcastically called it, offered more local news for our community on the southeast side. We were not much for TV, not sure if we even had one at that time. For a few years we did not have a TV because of a plant watering snafu, and my parents' inability to afford a new one. Even when we did have television, it was highly regulated in my childhood home.

Anyway, I asked my parents if I could cut out articles after they were done with the newspapers and they said yes, so I began gathering articles on science. Three to five articles were collected in about a week so I just kept clipping. My parents gave me a large manila envelope to put them in. I remember being really proud of my growing envelope. Our teacher was trying to show us that science was part of our everyday lives, and I certainly learned that and so much more.

On the ascribed due date, as we all filed past Mrs. Gruba into the classroom, I handed her my envelope. Her hands were otherwise empty, but I didn't give it much thought. When class began, Mrs. Gruba stood at the front of the room holding my envelope. She asked the class if anyone remembered her assignment to clip articles about science. The students seemed restless. She asked if anyone had any clippings to share, and no one raised a hand or motioned to indicate they had. Then she said something like, "Well, Amy remembered."

This, of course, made me super excited. I'm sure I was smiling proudly. She said she'd asked for a few, but I brought an entire envelope full and she began to go through them. She read the headlines and some of the articles aloud and the class discussed the science of it. Everyone seemed really engaged in the discussion of the articles. I was so happy my clippings were interesting to everyone. It felt great.

Then I got to recess. Two girls (both of whom became National Honor Society students in high school by the way) pulled me around the corner of the building, outside the view of any adults, and began punching me in the stomach, taking turns over and over. And when school was over, one of the girls lived near me, so she followed behind me until out of sight of the crossing guard and punched me in the stomach all the way down the block toward home. This went on for about a week.

Kids can be so mean. I doubt if Mrs. Gruba knew what she set me up for, but maybe. While a bad lesson was certainly instilled in me, perhaps I inspired my assailants to try harder in school. I have no idea where either girl is today and I feel no urge to look.

TRiCKS OF THE EGO

To live fully, you have to let go of your ego. It's a trickster if you let it be. One of the big Tricks of the Ego women especially are taught is holding onto youth. Another being taught through conditioning is that other women are your enemy or who you are competing against. If you are a tennis player, then that may be the case. In life, the only person we are competing against is ourselves. I know that sounds trite, but it isn't. You will never be happy or find any true joy if you are concerned with what other people have or believe you are in competition with anyone.

We are all in this together, and one of the key ways to subjugate a people is to divide and conquer, which is what western society has done to women. We are sisters, all of us. We are not competing for a man. We are not back stabbers. That stuff uses all of your good energy and real power in wastefulness, like throwing your clothes away every day. At some point, it is an illness. Gluttony of things is still gluttony.

Ladies, let's stop running each other down. If where you are is so bleak you have to fight another woman for a man, go somewhere else. Seriously. Move to Alaska or something. Move to a bigger city, a different town, wherever, you'll meet people.

Women are mutilating their bodies for the perfect boobs or ass cheeks, getting filler injected into their facess - it's bizarre to me. These are foreign bodies. Do they tell women that when you get breast implants you have to replace them every 10 to 15 years? That's a lot of surgery. I want to get through life without any surgeries if I can help it. Why would I get one that serves no medical purpose? If you are reading this with implants and filler and Botox and a face life under your belt, that's okay. You do you, but are you? I get it, I want to be "perfect" too. I'm not trying to tell people how to live, I'm figuring out how I want to live in the world. Change is slow.

I don't like medical procedures and want to have as few as possible, but I know people on their fifth, tenth, or twentieth surgery, on their knee, their elbow, maybe a tummy tuck, shoulder surgery. That's cool, that is your choice. That's the beauty of the world we live in, choice. I'm not telling you how to live, I'm saying explore why. Are you getting what you need out of life?

Love yourself as you are, as the beautiful person you are inside and out. None of the scars, sleeves, or accoutrements matter in the end. Our hearts and minds are where our true beauty lives. I am shaming no one. Adorned is captivating. Marking ourselves is ritual, I get it. I believe in reclaiming rites of passage. We have so few. Other cultures have elaborate ceremonies yet we have very little in that realm. But is it for you, for expansion of mind and body, or for something outside yourself like approval from others?

I am saying take a look at who you are, learn about yourself, and take care of yourself the way you need to. But love yourself however you are. Ego is a mighty power. Egomaniacs are the most insecure of people. The ego is friend and foe; watch after it with skepticism and question. Make sure you are living to your standards, in ways that serve you truly, and not being a slave to the ego and its trickery.

When I first found myself alone I was feeling ugly and unlovable, and I went to a cosmetic surgeon for a consultation. They suggested "filler", but no one could explain what was in it. Simply, silicone was injected under the cheek, and I could get it every two years. Or I could line up on Tuesdays for Botox shots for $300. None of that seemed right for me. I just got a facial instead.

OVERCOMiNG SOCiETAL BULLSHiT

I think I have said it before, and I am saying it again. As women, we have had a bunch of weird falsehoods and mutations forced upon our womanhood since the subjugation of women began. Many of them we don't even realize. The interpretations of so-called holy texts to control and demonize women, to deny women their power as creators, as healers, as teachers.

Women have been slaves of society chained by attitudes instead of bondage. What is allowed? What is proper? What is not allowed for a woman to do? Then there are the double standards of the sexes, even now. We have been taught to fear our menopause, to be ashamed of it. To Hell with that! I am embracing all of it.

The fact is, we have to turn our backs on societal rules. We lived by them long enough. Let go, celebrate you. Learn to love and care for yourself. Try new things. You are a limitless being! As society says, we are an invisible demographic, let's use that freedom to say goodbye to any societal rules, laws, expectations or traditions. We are not part of that nonsense any longer. We are free to explore... The world, ourselves, our hearts, the universe!

"Do Nothing Useless" says Henry Thomas Hamblin. He's right, leave all that bullshit aside. The time for idle chatter, carrying about the opinions of others, and standing aside due to societal bullshit is over!

CONTROLLiNG OUTCOMES

When I was in junior high, the school I went to was built on a wetlands. Marshes and such were and usually still are considered wasted land -- just sitting there being useless, and tragically man has little use for song birds, amphibians, and the slow filtration of our water. Doesn't seem to matter that the Earth in its wisdom has made everything perfect for us to exist and thrive. That doesn't stop us from trying to control nature. Again and again, mankind attempts to control nature, seldom considering the real devastation this has on the land and ultimately back on us.

Anyway, the school was built probably around the mid 1960s, and was mostly on a slab of concrete sitting atop the land, except for the gymnasium. The gym was built about six feet, or two meters, into the ground. Every year of the three years I attended junior high, the floor of the gymnasium would buckle in the Spring from the heavy Midwestern rains. All those April showers bringing May flowers would also cause the floor of the gym to be thrust up by swelling and moving dirt in the refusing to be tamed wetlands. Every year it happened, and every year our final few months of gym was all outside, rain or shine.

What a futile use of tax dollars, what a waste of resources and supplies, and what foolishness of man!!! Even at 13, I was stunned at the waste and the arrogance of it all. A yellow line of caution tape would suddenly be blocking the doors of the gym on some spring morning after a heavy rainfall.

That is exactly what it's like when we try to control outcomes in relationships and situations in our lives.

To attempt to control the actions or feeling of others is impossible. The sooner we recognize this for ourselves, the better. I do not have children, but I can see most of the conflict between parents and children is parents still trying to control outcomes in the lives of their children as adults. It makes sense to control the situation when your kid is nine, but not at 39. All one can do is offer the tools for successful living to our children or young people in our lives and hope they make good use of them. Sure, be there as a support, but don't try to be there as a warden.

Wanting to control outcomes creeps out in a variety of unhealthy ways in our lives. I finally saw it in the way I would overdo kindness sometimes, either by doing more than I could afford, or over obligating myself to my own detriment, or by acting in an exaggerated manner to ensure people would like me. For example if invited to a potluck, I would want to make not one, not two, but three kinds of cookies. Beyond my love of baking, it was because I didn't feel good about myself and needed to overdo it so people wouldn't see how I was lacking or dirty or bad. Of course, I wasn't lacking or dirty or bad, I just believed I was. All that was in my head. Nobody liked me better if I brought three kinds of cookies instead of one. I could have brought a store bought coffeecake and no one would like me better or worse for it. That was the control I was holding onto though, out of feelings of not being enough. Wanting to control situations is foolish - it's foolish because it is impossible.

Sending a thank you note after a gift was received, or after a job interview, isn't trying to control a situation, it's being proper and polite. Giving a gift with strings attached is control. We cannot make people love us. We cannot buy control. Not even the federal government can buy our control. They may think they can, but we are the same as that swirling marsh, always bubbling up.

If you need to work out some control issues, maybe try it in some BDSM scenario? I do not say that flippantly; I am serious. There is a reason bondage is practiced in this modern world. Like therapy, bondage can be a course of treatment with an ending when healed, or maybe it becomes a lifelong practice like meditation or yoga?

Maybe meditate on it and try to understand why you are focusing on others instead of yourself. We are the only things in our life that we have control over. That's it, just us.

We can't fix the outside if we can't fix the inside. What are you doing to fix things? Sometimes all it takes is a little thankfulness. What gifts and beauty around you are you overlooking? We have this time, this life. What are we doing with it?

MAKE NO TiME FOR REGRET

"Regrets, I've had a few, but then again, too few to mention..."

If only we all felt the way Frank Sinatra did in that lyric. Regret is a powerful poison. It keeps us from fully appreciating our past, and refuses to allow us to enjoy the present moment. The past is gone, there is no way to redo past mistakes. Regret about our actions, missed opportunities, or poor decisions are fixed items in our personal histories. They shaped part of who we are. They cannot be undone, but we can use them to learn and grow.

If we allow ourselves to explore deeply the why of those events we regret, we can glean a much deeper understanding of our fears and weaknesses. Maybe even turn them into strengths.

At this point in life, yeah, you probably have a few regrets. So it goes. Funny thing about life: it is short and it is long. Living in regret will make these days dreary and long. Why do that to yourself? Flogging ourselves for a mistake, a moment of malice, or even a lifetime of deceit does nothing to improve the quality of our lives today. The past is gone. Sure, in some quantum leap we could go back and right wrongs, but how would that change other things in our lives? Instead, maybe we need to take responsibility, accept it, and move on to greener pastures.

Some months after my marriage ended, I became overcome with regret. Why didn't I leave long ago? But through a particularly powerful meditation in the backyard one day, I realized in every instance of "why didn't I leave then?" there was some amazing experience or incredible person I met afterward that likely would not have occurred if I had left. I was able to let go of my regrets and appreciate all the wonderful moments of my life during marriage. Moreover, I was able to embrace the present with a vigor of optimism like never before. It made me realize how useless an emotion regret is.

Regret isn't going to resurrect anyone from the dead. It's not going to change the past. In fact, it is going to create more and more regret as time goes on if we sit in the past thinking of our failings rather than living in the now and changing our attitudes and behaviors.

Regrets, if we learn from them and let them go, can become our greatest teachers and help us manifest the power to make the present and future a million times better. Have regrets? Ask yourself how you can fix them? How can you insure there are not more similar regrets in today and tomorrow?

When I looked at my own regrets, most were less about the things I had done and more about the things I had not done. Times when I knew better and went against my instincts, opportunities I lacked the courage to jump on, or the road not taken due to fear.

Now, I can live in those regrets, dwelling on opportunities missed, or I can move forward and live. I can learn from those past mistakes and use them to make better choices today. Today, I will not compromise on my own goals. Today, I will not put others before myself. Today, I try not to be penny-wise and pound foolish.

I know people who have reached the last quarter in life and their lives are nothing but regrets. How terrible, how sorrowful! Nothing good can come our way if we are filled with regret, no positive outcomes, no worthwhile opportunities, because we are cloaked in the veil of negativity. To hell with that!!!

Open your eyes and see that regret is a fool's game. It is a living death. It is one of the most useless emotions out there. Learn from your mistakes and move on. Embrace the future, welcome new opportunities. Make good if you wronged someone. You are still alive today, act like it, and release yourself from the bondage of regret.

EXPECTATION IS THE KILLER OF JOY

Expectation is a human failure we all fall prey to sometimes. Remember the birthday as a kid when you thought for sure you'd get that dream gift, but you didn't? You probably still received lovely things, still had a nice cake, people wishing you a good day, but you were so bummed about what you didn't get, you could not have a good time. We've all done it. But, the problem of your disappointment never really fell on whoever failed to procure the desired gift. It was your expectation that did you in.

If we let go of expectations, we can enjoy much more happiness in life. Expectation is the killer of joy. That statement freed me from a lot of useless worry. Moreover, it removed any level of measurement from my experiences. We have to let things unfold sometimes and simply be in the moment, not in our heads.

It was a realization I had a few years ago, after a couple of friends visited for a holiday. I went to extremes to make it fun because the holidays are hard for some people. I was used to doing random elaborate celebrations to help thwart holiday blues for my former partner, so in my limited budget way, I went all out.

One of the friends was a total ingrate about the whole thing. The visit started to have this whole "mean girls" vibe to it, and I was the odd one out. It really hurt my feelings. If someone wants to be unpleasant about a person trying hard to make something festive, that is certainly their choice. My feelings being hurt was my choice. I am in no way suggesting bad behavior should be endured, but we let ourselves down by expecting behavior.

Thinking about it a month or so later, I realized that I had been carrying an expectation about the weekend, that my two guests would be as committed to a good time as I was. I expected there might be a gift exchange of some kind, so I had little things for each of them. Instead, everything went sideways. I realized that all that pain and hurt was based on my expectations of how the weekend would go versus how it went. If I had no expectations, then the one person's nasty behavior could have been shrugged off, ignored, or dealt with in some more positive manner. Instead I was hurt.

In Buddhism, they say attachment causes suffering, meaning everything we love goes away, until we go away, but expectation is right there with it. Having a goal one doesn't achieve creates suffering. Why? Because we had an expectation. We played out a fantasy scenario in our head about how things were going to go, and it didn't, and now we are suffering. For example, putting weight on holidays like Valentine's Day to measure your relationship by. Someone has expectations, maybe unrealistic expectations about how it will unfold, then they are angry when it goes a different way.

We cannot control the outcome of a given situation. We can prepare for and work toward the results we want, but that's where our control ends.

If we go into a situation with any preconceived ideas about how it's going to be, obviously aside from a positive outlook, we are probably going to be disappointed. Predicting the actions of others is futile, and serves no good purpose. We cannot know nor control what another outside of us is thinking or how they may act. If you find yourself disappointed with various endeavors, isn't it usually your expectations that were to blame?

Having expectations is not the same as having goals. We should always have goals ahead of us, in various facets of our lives, and multiple overlapping goals indeed! It's when we try to predict the future or know others actions that we get ourselves into trouble. We can only predict how we ourselves act out in the world, and even that can be a surprise. Trying to know what someone outside of us is going to do is futile. Sure, we get a feeling, we have intuition, and maybe even a psychic vision, but anything can happen. In my example, I went beyond merely having the goal of a good time over a holiday and began to imagine scenarios.

Expectation is not the same as wonder. Wonder is meaningful, it is standing on the precipice of this *Great Is All* that we are all inside of. Wonder can be in a pursuit or a study, a walk on the beach, or a hike up to a majestic overlook.

I understand the idea that expectation can be a negative thing may go against everything you know about thinking positive or working toward a goal. We are told to "expect the best", and damn well we should! Having expectations about what that best will be, is something else. Expecting the best and having expectations are two entirely different things.

Think of all the people who study some subject to high honors and degrees only to find they hate working in that field and have some other passion. Often it was their expectation of what the profession and their career would be like rather than what it really was that ruined it for them. Maybe they could have found some niche they liked, but they didn't, or perhaps they became disillusioned. Or they moved on to something else entirely, sometimes to great success. Sometimes to ruin.

Expectation is arrogance. Expectation is wanting to control aspects of an outcome that we cannot know until it happens. Expectation is something we affix to others or situations, but we only really have control over ourselves, our actions, and our reactions. When we think we know how something is going to turn out, rather than allowing for the blank slate of letting it unfold, we harm our joy.

This isn't about not planning; it's about not worrying. It is not creating fairy tales and fantasy scenarios in our heads and then being upset when they do not happen. Let the world unfold. Forcing things almost never works out.

WORRY IS A FAILED STATE

I've spoken about fear; the other side of that bad coin is worry. Worry, I have come to realize, is just selfishness wrapped in tissue paper. In Manly P. Hall's timeless 'Ten Basic Rules for Better Living' from 1953, he says, "Do not confuse thoughtfulness with worry."

Indeed!

His words are so true. Worrying about stuff doesn't fix anything, we have to channel it into good action or let it go. I realized that I spent so much time worrying, and what ever came of it? It became a paralysis of action. I needed money for bills, if I worried it never made money appear. If I proactively did something - anything; it could flow right in.

What was the use of fretting then? Just a selfish waste of time. When I looked at it as the deficit it was, it allowed me to realize worry is a failed state of being.

I decided worry was doing me no good. Sure, we all worry sometimes, but most of our worries are foolishness. A 2019 Penn State study reported 91% of our worries are really false alarms. Other studies peg needless worry at 85% to 97% of all worrying. Worrying is a waste of precious time, action is what is needed, not hand wringing. No matter if it's a false alarm or a real concern, worry fixes nothing.

As a radical solution, I decided to practice not worrying, never worrying - even with the things I should or could worry about, the "real" worries. Worry is anti-magic for solving problems. Worry is like having ink in our eyes when looking for solutions, so I said "No More!" And I quit, cold turkey.

As far as feeling worry since I've given it up, if I do it is momentary. I just acknowledge it and move forward. "Ever forward, never straight ahead", as the guys I hung with in high school would say about driving instructions. If I catch myself worrying I try to do something physical for a few minutes, yard work or yoga.

What is the point of worrying? There is no point.

We can be so afraid and insecure that worry becomes a joy buzzer of negative energy. Worry becomes an addiction like caffeine. We love it, we revel in it. It's the American way, to lie awake at night and worry. We worry about bills, and the future in this mad world, about tomorrow's sales meeting, or affording college for our kids, or how is your mom going to survive burdensome medical debt? I bet most of us don't know life without the pit of worry in our stomachs. We have a lot to worry about certainly, if we want to.

Ever forward. To worry fixes no problem.

Do I have legitimate big deal reasons to worry? Absolutely I do. Right now especially, but worry serves no purpose. Planning, action, and forward momentum are the only things that will help, not standing still in fear.

I caught myself the other day on the phone. I said to a friend, "I worry about..." I caught it mid-sentence. My lazy choice of words, my error invoking the terrible word "worry". I do not worry. I ponder, I question, I research, but I do not worry. To consciously avoid worrying, I need to more carefully choose my words, because our words have power.

Which is a perfect segue into the next thing I want to mention, and that is our words and our intent, as I used them in my "Universe Experiments".

UNiVERSE EXPERiMENTS

Sometimes in life I have learned we just have to "give it to the universe". Things can appear pretty bleak sometimes. Hopeless, even. Times can be hard. At those times I might look to the moon, the sun, or a star, whatever I can find, and I ask the universe, the power of the universe, to help me through, to find a solution where none exists, for the best outcome. And so many times, the universe unfolds to assist.

The universe, whatever it is, if it's real or a simulation, is powerful at least in our minds from what we have been taught. We understand the universe as the vast darkness, the unknown, expansive to infinity, and hiding answers to so many mysteries in its distant spaces. It is the black nothingness some dream of exploring. All of that gives it power in our own minds.

Any readers of faith who worship Jesus, or Allah, or God are probably shouting at me right now that it's their deity, not the universe. I think we are all done sitting at the kid's table at holidays, so can we please admit that it's all the same? We just put different names on it. You have your deity, your neighbor has theirs, I have mine. Call it want you want, Deity #42. For me it's the Power of the Universe, the energy of life.

"Giving it to the universe" as I call it, has worked for me many times in life as I look, but I seem to forget that this is often the best thing to do. It frees us from worry, fear, and expectation - the worst of demons. On the surface it may sound rudderless and lacking in planning, but that is not the case. We should always we working off a plan of goals and working to get there, but we have to let go of the How and focus on the Why.

No better example of this was years ago on a road trip. It was the kind of trip that is all journey and no destination. The trip was going all ways sideways, and things got desperate. The more we tried to make it happen, the worse it got. Finally in my frustration I announced to the sky, "That's it, I give up! It's up to the road to provide. I am giving it to the road!" I uttered those words, I took it as truth, and poof! Everything started falling into place. Amazing new opportunities opened up to us, and the road did indeed provide! I was in awe of the power!

The trip was a year-long road trip I was on with my former husband, dog, and turtle. It was essentially dressed up homelessness, but we really made the most of it. In fact, in the end we had the most amazing experiences and met the most incredible people! Our plan was to work our way around the country and document the people we met and the experiences we had. We slept in the car at rest stops, stayed with friends or kind strangers. We produced an vast amount of content - hours of great video footage that became hundreds of short videos on YouTube, interviews, photos, journal posts, plus producing a book and a documentary film after it was over.

We began with $180 between us, a laptop computer, a video camera, and a Chevy Blazer. It was not the best circumstances. Early on in the trip, it seemed the more we tried to force things the worse it got. At some point we were flat broke with nowhere to go and no way to move forward.

In deep desperation, I finally proclaimed those magic words, that I was leaving it to the road and almost instantaneously the road provided. Truth is truth, a thousand philosophers before me have come to the same conclusion. That if we open to life, to the universe, to god, gods, or whomever, it is amazing! If we let things unfold, if we follow our path, the world will open to us.

I have learned well the power of words and intent, especially within ourselves and between ourselves and the universe. Shortly after my husband left, I was having a particularly bad day, and in my grief I said "What else could go wrong?" And boy howdy! I learned a lot that day, lots of stuff could go wrong and did! I took it back as quickly as I could.

As I sat in the bathroom at my job, my face in my hands. I suddenly had the thought, "If asking that could make worse things happen, then couldn't then saying the opposite also be true???"

While journaling on that thought later that night, I remembered that road trip project years back, and how announcing I was "giving it to the road" - forcing myself to shed my fear and frustration seemed to almost instantly turn things our way. Connections came together, new opportunities appeared, the day was saved, and things moved along, over and over.

As I adjusted to my new reality of being on my own, I began to try "Universe Experiments". When things got rough, or if I was afraid, I would ask the universe for help, or rather, I would "Leave it up to the Universe". I'd tell myself it was going to work out great, and things started to. I'd tell myself "Something good is going to happen today", and viola! Something good would happen. Sure, some were small things, but still, I was counting. I needed to turn things around if I was going to survive the heartache of my breakup.

Every day after I said affirmations and welcomed good things to come my way, and it was coming true! Once I envisioned what I needed, there it was! It was unbelievable. The more positive I told myself my day was going to be, it was. Sure, some days the "bad guys" won, but 90% of the time if I looked to the best I received the best, in amazing and unexpected ways! Welcome opportunity and it knocks on the door!

Did bad things happen too? Well yeah, it's life, but I chose to look for the good aspects of my changing circumstance as much as I could muster. Usually these days, if things start going wrong in my day, I can identify if there is some fear-based muscle memory creeping up, or if I am over extending myself, or getting my boundaries pushed. If I step back for a moment, I can see it and change it. If we stop and separate ourselves for a moment from the moment, we can solve a lot of our problems, and let go of the things we have no control over.

The Universe Experiments have been life changing. It has taught me a lot about myself, and about just how powerful thoughts can be. When we think the worst, we get the worst, when we think for the best, the best happens. It can be miraculous sometimes. Poof!

Time and time again, things would work out and magical events unfolded before my eyes. At the worst moments in life I have tried to stay positive and look to the best. Often circumstances have righted themselves with miraculous opportunities and experiences.

Not long after writing about my Universe Experiments and the power of words, I stumbled upon this interesting woman named Florence Scoval Shinn. She was an illustrator and new age author in the 1920s. She had all these fun ways of saying things that were little chants or mantras for success. So in regard to Universe Experiments, her version was something like this: "I give to the divinity inside me and I go free". I like that too.

SURVIVING OLD AGE IN A STRANGE WORLD -- OR WHERE ARE YOU HUNKERING DOWN?

With all the changes happening to us physically, and all the important things we should be considering, one aspect I don't want to overlook here is a most important one: Survival.

In seventh grade, my English teacher Mr. Jackson announced to the class that we would be the first generation of Americans not to do as good as, or better than our parents. Prophetic bastard! But it was easy to see with the closing of nearly all the local steel mills just a few years earlier and the stolen pensions of the mill's retirees.

I'm going to bet few of my generation are enjoying pensions. When I entered the work world in the late 1980s, the idea of pensions was pretty much a pipe dream, something from the past. A short lived past. Two generations? Pensions had moved on to the early 401k, which were basically at that time a gift to the employers. My first full-time job offered a 401k, but in their early era, if you didn't retire from that company, it just folded back into the company. You got nothing if you left before retirement. I recall it was 3% from the company, but after a couple years, when I left at the ripe old age of 21, I didn't get any check in the mail. I got nothing, zip. That money rolled right back into the company I worked for.

I had a 401k from another more recent job, but I used half of it as the down payment on the house I'm sitting in, and the other half got spent on survival after that position ended. Retirement day is never coming for most of us if everything stays on today's trajectory.

I can only speak for myself here, but staying afloat has been challenging through my entire adult life. Recently I came across some old tax returns. From 2010 to 2013, I made $12,000 to $15,000, and I was the bread winner!

My own parents never really reached into middle class, we were "upper low class" as I called it. I've been middle class, lower middle class that is, for maybe three years of my adult life, and I was working myself to death to do it. How will I keep up that kind of workload when I'm 75? I'm not. Are you?

Then there is peak earning time in our life, which appears to be mid 30s to about 50. After that, if you are in the corporate world, you better have been moved to the corner office by now or you are going down, down, down. And, if you are a person in the trades or a laborer, how many years does one have in that? They are supposed to be retiring at 55. Worse even, is trying to change jobs after 50. We are pretty much obsolete in the eyes of most companies, everyone wants a shiny new Gen Y or Z.

In my brief stint in corporate work, it was easy to see my generation, Gen X was getting quashed. The Boomers refused to retire, holding on for more, and probably afraid for their own future. When they finally did retire, they were replaced with Millennials, not us - not Gen X. A "fresh perspective", don't you know? I realized then, we were the generation that would be leap-frogged.

Not to say it's any better for the generations coming after us. When a person has $100,000 in student loan debt and they are fighting for a job that pays $48k a year, and their rent is $2000 a month, they are pretty much fucked. Pardon my words there, but it's true. It's how it ever was, but not. It's gotten steadily worse. Yes, my father had two jobs and my mother worked part-time, but it wasn't the desperate struggle of today. I'm not being a downer, but the system in place is not going to work for us, so we better figure it out before too long.

If every problem of a society is systemic, then it's time we create something new. Did you know there used to be laws that only people could buy houses, not corporations? That's what kept home prices low. Neighborhoods could accommodate nearly any family into affordable home ownership - black and white, poor and middle class. Home ownership helped build the middle class; it's not the other way around.

In 2020, while we were dealing with the lockdown disaster, a few companies went around buying up 100,000 single family homes a week. I'm not being a conspiracy nut here; it's documented. The New York Times called it a "$60 billion housing grab" (10-22, 2021). This isn't new. This is gentrification at its core. Developers inflating real estate values to get people priced out, taxed out, and unable to pass family property down to the next generation.

Recently, a friend put his mother in assisted living. It was $3500 a month just for the rent. It went up to $8,000 per month if she needed assistance of any sort, such as simple medicine administration, and I hear from others that this is considered cheap! When the current base monthly pay of Social Security is $700 a month, how does that work?

Another friend recently sent me a video of an American woman living her best life in Mexico. The woman says she loves it and it's where she can afford to live. A former coworker of mine and her husband moved to Mexico some years back because his $700 a month social security check was unable to sustain him anywhere in the USA. When they were here, the wife worked full-time. The husband had the aforementioned $700 social security "entitlement windfall". They both had part-time jobs too, just for ends to meet. Now they play ukulele on the beach in Mexico and his social security income covers all of their bills.

It's a beautiful notion. Of course we should all go live in a foreign land for retirement if we want to, or any time for that matter, but let's face it -- we shouldn't HAVE to go. We as Americans should be able to sustain in America in our golden years without having a million dollars in the bank, and without living in a tent, or eating cat food.

I am optimistic. I believe if we put our heads together we could stop playing "their" game, and create something better. But we keep feeding in. Today it's bit oin and "flipping houses", before that it was the stock market and building giant houses in the burbs. Before that maybe gold prospecting? It's always something. Now we are being played to believe we want tiny homes and van life. After all, the cute girl with 400k followers on social media says it's her best life. I suspect these are all paid actors, because social media is the new TV. But hey, what do I know?

Until we stand up together and demand a different way of life we are never going to get it. Housing should be affordable for all a nation's citizens, it is a human right. When I rented my first apartment in 1988, I was told by the landlords and rental agents that I could only rent a place that was up to 30% of my income. They only showed me places in that price range, which amounted to a bunch of crazy studio apartments, but I was able to pay my bills. How many of you are spending a mere 30% of your pay on your housing now? Not me, that is for sure. In fact, when I bought this house with an FHA loan I could go to 50% of my income or more. How does that work? What that tells me is consumer protection does not exist in today's world. It shows something is really wrong in this state of the union and elsewhere.

In China, they tore up farmland and built huge cities with bullet trains to commute. But no one in China could afford the prices of the apartments, and now they are demolishing them. All in the name of progress. So much waste of resources! The government of China probably could have gifted a nice apartment in one of those cities to every person living in poverty in other overcrowded cities, and then no one would be living in a hovel. They could pay them to move there for a period of time and settle in, build a community, start businesses, and offer some way to buy it eventually as they get on their feet, even via sweat equity. This could have created pride of ownership for them, changing their lives for generations. But instead of any such thing for the good of the nation and the people, they let the buildings and entire cities rot.

We in the USA have bulldozed every meadow, every marsh, to build subdivisions devoid of anything - no character, ugly boxes in shades of beige. They cut all the big trees, replacing them with spindly starts, creating entire communities without a single bit of shade. Often these so-called "neighborhoods" offer no sidewalks or real services, and nothing in walking distance. Builders keep building faster and cheaper houses, yet millions of homes sit empty. None of it makes sense. When we constantly mix progress and "bottom line thinking", nothing good can happen.

We can do better!

We need to be creative about housing in the very near future. I recall a meme a few years back that said something like 'Seven women buy a mansion together for their old age'. That is an option, I am all for being creative. Do we buy an old house in a dead farming town and make it co-living? Do we buy land and build small structures and a farm for off grid living in some remote part of the US? I'm not sure if I'm a farmer, I've been a gardener fairly successfully sometimes, and not very well other times. Hard to depend soley on oneself, also challenging is finding others to share with.

Communal living isn't right for everyone. Do we move in with our kids? Certainly there was a time when most households in America and everywhere were multi-generational, it's probably a lot healthier, but that's not for everyone either, I for one don't have kids, nor much family. Those are some possible options. Maybe we could look back at visionaries like Buckminster Fuller, Nikola Tesla, or earthship creator Michael Reynolds and adapt some ideas. Perhaps building more structures like earth ships, adobes and cob houses with available material is a solution? What do you have?

But again, why can't I stay in my house? How is it that to have an affordable retirement we all have to get in groups, or move to the middle of nowhere, or become expats? Instead, I bet if we brainstormed a bit, we could find a way to demand better from this nation of ours. Making that happen requires determination, time to spend on solving the problems, visionary solutions, and it requires us to use our days for something important, maybe something bigger than we are individually.

If we are to "Be The Orca, how do we do that? It might be time to stand up and be counted!

We need to get ready with ideas and plans. What if we demanded housing prices settle back to a realistic level? And obviously if we are going there, we need to tackle employers paying correctly, putting wages where they should be. And let's make our social safety nets stronger and better to raise people up who need it, so we all can succeed. There are so many ills to tackle, from poverty to protecting nature; from cleaning our waterways to campaign reform to allow for REAL representation of the people; from dismantling monopolies and removing the existence of billionaires to cleaning toxic waste dumps and resolving our trash problem. There is so much, but if we stand and demand in unity to tackle these things, it can happen.

Does that sound all pie in the sky? It shouldn't. Being able to live somewhere throughout our lives is really a bare minimum of a thriving civilization. Seeing a dentist if your tooth hurts should not be the difference between a home or not. Wealth disparity is the typical end of nearly every civilization throughout history. If that day has come, we need to stand up and take the lead.

The system and our government will bend to the will of the people. If enough people want it, it has to happen. One recent example is gay marriage. While the media refused to cover it, the LGBTQ community came together, hundreds of thousands of people strong at the capital. They forced the issue, and things moved quickly.

If we want to thrive for all of our lives, then we have a duty to ourselves and to all others to create a just and compassionate world. It will never be perfect, but we can certainly do better than this current situation. We could easily demonstrate our power with a general strike or other actions. I don't mean armchair protest and petitions, I mean putting our collective foot down, and saying enough is enough. It's about the future, yours and mine, and there is no time to delay.

IDLE HANDS = BRAIN DEATH

Idleness is death. When we stop learning or growing, we die. We have all heard stories about the man who retires after 40 years on the job, and drops dead from boredom a month later because he doesn't know what to do with his time.

I have to be honest: I have a hard time understanding boredom. Do people really get bored?

Recently, a scary winter storm trapped me in my house for more than a week. I got a little stir crazy because I usually walk with my dog every morning but it was impossible to leave the yard due to the slick ice sheet covering everything outside my door for days and days. I was scared some of the time, and I did worry a bit, but I was never bored. I made art, I wrote, I worked on some cleaning projects. Talked with the dog and turtle, and a few friends on the phone. I don't think I once got bored.

Boredom fits in somewhere, as a momentary feeling to alert us to possible stagnation, but it's not a state of being. Can you ever have done everything you are interested in? Could there really be nothing bringing you joy? I feel like boredom is a lack of joy and wonder. It's tragic. It's sadly astonishing how many people turn to meth in their forties and fifties, or drink themselves to death out of boredom. But why? How? It's hard to fathom.

I've been overworked, fearful, exhausted, delighted, angry, exasperated, had feelings of futility, but I don't remember ever being bored. It's a state of mind I think. If things become commonplace or drudgery sets in, I always work to change my situation. I'm not going to stand for boredom. There is always something new to learn or try, or something we enjoy to revisit. A few kind words with someone at the gas station, or a friendly exchange on the beach can inspire something amazing. Life is packed with incredible beauty and magical moments if we would just open our eyes to the world around us.

I understand we can get beaten down by life. It can be brutal, but in those times finding new joys, even small joys is even more vital. I was recently at a park and an eagle slowly circled by. In my excitement I blurted out, "Did you see that?" to a group of young men, all buried in their phones. "An eagle just flew over." I could see childlike wonder spread across each of their faces in that moment, all looking up to search the sky for it, ending what had a moment before been blank stares into their palms. Now they were taking in the moment and the location they were in.

When there begins to be some drudgery in life I always change up my routine. I'll try something new, learn a new skill, or volunteer in a new way in my community. There is always something to be done, some new way to feed my soul.

I spent two years living north of the Iron Range in rural northern Minnesota. Two winters, easily six months long, and often more than 25 degrees below zero. During the second winter, my husband was away for six weeks. My canine companion Cheyenne and I embarked on a goal to run across a very frozen Miner's Lake. There was a tall rock wall on the other side, it was an old iron ore pit mine that had struck water and was now a lake, stocked with fish annually by the Department Of Natural Resources.

The temperature being so cold, we could only be outside for about an hour even in the daylight. These were wilds, there were moose, wolves, coyotes, cougar and bear. It was not a place to be irresponsible, especially if it was 40 below. There were special clothes and boots required up there, and most cars and trucks had electric plugs hanging out of the front of the grill. These were for battery warmers around your car battery so it would start up in the freezing cold. Thinking about it now, we were crazy to be out walking some of those times!

I had no idea what we were really getting into, the cliff wall on the other side of the lake didn't look far, but once we passed most of the ice fishing houses dotting the snow covered ice, the cliff was still in the distance. It was going to take some time. It took us more than a month of daily walks to work our way over to touch the wall. It was so much further, and so much taller than we, (rather I), had ever imagined. I can't speak for Cheyenne, I'm sure she was quite aware!

But the thing was, I never got bored. I found things to do. I watched a bunch of old movies from the 1930s and '40s, which was a great education in pre-formula Hollywood when dialogue instead of constant action was the bulk of a film. I read, I wrote, and I did a bunch of baking.

Some people get older and start drinking heavily, or eating bad, or being sedentary. It's a slow suicide. Processed food in America is mostly poison. I've experienced it myself, eating white bread or store bought cookies or doughnuts, then felt them affecting my mood and behavior almost instantly, becoming irritable, angry, and maybe even a little paranoid.

We put far too much faith in government, in the medical industrial complex, and big business to be ethical and honorable. Sure, that is how it should be, but not how it is. None have our best interest at heart. Only when the people stand together and demand change does anything change. These are issues that bother me. I hate injustice. I don't want to support the war machine. You have your own subjects that mean a lot to you. Consider them carefully. How can you help something you believe in? If politics isn't your thing, maybe it's cleaning the shoreline, or protecting and nurturing trees and open spaces, or being a foster parent?

If you are one of those people counting down to retirement with fear and dread, and you just can't imagine not doing whatever you do for a living, then start doing new things immediately. If you have a handful of years left to work, start doing something new tomorrow. Sign up for a course to learn something you always wanted to know more about -- stained glass, geology, herbal medicine. Get a spiral notebook and spend 30 minutes a day researching some subject you want to know more about, make notes. Maybe it can turn into something later? Maybe you'll end up knowing a bunch about gemstones, or the dadaists, or the life of urban squirrels and raccoons. There's a million things. Those are just some of my interests, I don't know what you are into.

I'd like to document all the Sears & Roebuck houses around today if I had the time. Do young people even know about those? Do people know that a whole beautiful house, a real house, could come as a kit? Not some 3-D printed square shed, but a real house! Fascinating! What do you got? What are you curious about?

My problem is the opposite of boredom. There are so many things I want to do, sometimes my ideas fall over themselves. I try to garden and go for walks in nature. I make art, I write, I have friends I try to spend time with. I work sporadic labor gigs right now, and I do freelance design and consulting. Which all sounds a lot cooler than it is. It's a lot of struggle.

There is no time or place for idle hands or minds, no matter what condition we are in. There is a journalist still writing a weekly column using only his eyes and a computer sensor because a tragic accident left him a quadriplegic. Think of Stephen Hawking pondering the mysteries of the universe from his wheelchair.

Right now I am still able-bodied. Maybe someday that will be harder, but even then there is more we can do. I remember seeing photos of Manet making art in his bed. He refused to be bored. Even sick and old and in bed, he kept creating. I know a wonderful woman who was stuck inside recovering from surgery and used the time to write postcards to politicians and other people in her community to try to effect change. I know we all are not going to agree on what is an important cause. I'll try to avoid things that divide, and shine a light where we can come together. Start with kindness, always be aware of kindness first.

Remember that the things we agree on are forever. They are bigger and more important than any of the divisive issues the media controls us with. It's simple. Everybody wants to have a good life. I believe I deserve that and so do you, and everyone else. We all want fresh air, clean water, real food, a roof over our head, the feeling of being part of a community, and the freedom to pursue our happiness.

We could lift the planet out of poverty, fix pollution, and find creative solutions to the major problems facing us all, if we just came together. We don't need the pike worthy brains of billionaires to save us. They can blast off to Mars. In fact please go. We can learn useful skills to share, we can learn to heal, or build, or help in some other way. The place could be a paradise if we got together and stopped being played by the media, bureaucracy, and our corporate masters. Think of the powerful message of Alan Moore's 'V for Vendetta'. The powers will run amok if we the people don't keep them in check.

A friend told me a while ago, "if you're not green you are not growing". He had a taken a gig in his field that was considered lesser than his usual position. He works in the movie and entertainment industry, and during the pandemic things were really slow. He needed money and was offered a gig doing something totally outside his usual line of work but still on the set. He told me over dim sum how much he was loving it because while he was still on set he was doing a totally different gig, and getting a completely new perspective on everything. Though not as high paying, he was learning new stuff every single day, and he could potentially use these new skills again in the future. He has a really good attitude about life. Someone else might have turned down the work as too low, or complained about it, but not him. He knows what bad times are. If you understand how difficult life can be, you tend to have a lot of compassion and a cheery disposition.

We are not the old of our grandparents, we are the old of today. We "still have miles to go before we sleep", to borrow from Robert Frost's famous poem. It is true, and we'd best enjoy it. If we chose to idle, bad things do happen. Having nothing to do is a stoppage of living, a living death. It is a sorrowful lack of secondary interests and goals.

Recently, a man in the laundromat told me he was 68 and bored. I asked if he traveled. He said he and his wife traveled extensively, and were just back from an international trek in fact, but it was boring. I was fascinated. I asked questions for my entire wash cycle, trying to understand how this man with world travels under his belt, freedom of time, and the income or savings to enjoy his leisure, could say he was bored. He looked gray and miserable indeed. He said, "I've done it all and seen everything I wanted to see". No matter how I pointed out his good fortune, he did not care. He did not see it as good or fortunate at all. It was intriguing to me, disturbingly intriguing.

Take for example, my own mother, who passed just a few short years ago. She barely left the house and seldom traveled, but when she did she was like a giddy school girl. Imagine if she'd had the opportunity to spend 15 years traveling the world - would she be bored? Would she become jaded in her adventures? I could not image that at all. How does someone lose their wonder of the world? My heart ached that my sweet mum did not have such opportunities while another could squander their joy so vehemently.

I have a strange feeling the man in the laundromat was bored because he wanted to be bored, or because marketing had told him he ought to be bored. There I go with marketing again. But honestly, how much of the symptoms of old age are taught to us by popular culture or TV, or come from something else entirely, like unprocessed trauma?

I may have mentioned that I have a friend whose mother is suffering from dementia. It is a tragic illness, and so little is known, even the best medicines available provide little help. Perhaps the reason it doesn't respond to medicine is because it comes from unprocessed trauma more than aluminum exposure, or as much anyway. The fact that dementia is epidemic in America says there is an underlying cause, either environmental, (perhaps medicine interactions), or not to sound paranoid, by design.

Maybe dementia is sadly visited upon those who stopped having goals, or being active, or who did not pursue some important dream because they lost contact with their inner child. I hate to sound all new age, but that inner child healing is real. We all learn some amount of misinformation as children and it colors our actions and thinking sometimes. Not being able to face our demons or our shadow creates a sad fading away of who we are.

When my father suffered a series of small strokes years ago, I did a lot of research on healing the brain. The power of our brain to heal and rewire itself is absolutely remarkable. If only we could utilize all of its full potential, we could probably fly, and maybe live forever. Anyway, I learned in China they use psychedelic and other mushrooms to treat dementia with much better success than the drugs used here. Is that because we know so little about the power of mushrooms and what they unlock, or is it because it pushes the user to let go of trauma and mange emotions such as grief in positive ways? Or both?

We need stimulation, and our brains need stimulation. We need it like we need oxygen. Don't deny yourself. Don't believe you can't start over, or find new joys or a new career. Don't fear change. Change is inevitable. Embrace it, find new things to learn, do, and experience. Why would you idle away? Take time to think about what you would like to do, or what you always wanted to do but never had time for. Or maybe that thing that scares you a bit. Don't regret or don't let fear hold you back. Try a dozen things, something will stick.

The number one regret of dying people is not trying that thing they dreamed of, letting fear hold them back from really living. If you had six months to live, what would you do? Do that! Live like that every day!

THE FREEDOM OF TODAY - WE ARE LiMiTLESS!

The biggest epiphany I had as my period became more sporadic was that I was no longer an important part of society. Women of child bearing age, young sexy women, and mothers were what mattered. I was now outside of that spectrum. Society suddenly had no use for me. I was invisible and unimportant. For a moment it made me sad and regretful, and then it dawned on me that this was freedom. Total freedom!

If I was no longer considered young and attractive, then I suddenly had a lot less to worry about. If I could no longer be considered for breeding, then I had the freedom to be an all-mother -- even my own mother! And, sex was now fully for pleasure! If society deemed me useless, I now had the freedom to embrace anything and everything!

I was suddenly without any obligation to look or act any part, and as women we are pigeon-holed from early life to be Everything, all the things - a princess, an angel, a mother, a nurse, a prostitute, a superhero, and an "independent" woman - and now I was Nothing. But nothingness is vital to the existence of the universe! Space is a vast nothingness, and we all look at outer space with awe. Nothingness is maybe a new kind of somethingness? That's what physics says. Nothingness is where the invisible happens. It is where magic and energy dance.

I have no traditions to follow anymore. My parents are both passed, my husband left, and I have no children to concern over. This gave me freedom from holidays, from duties and obligations to others that maybe didn't serve me - all the stress people experience at Christmas for example. I like sending gifts to people because I was thinking about them, not because of a holiday that says I should.

I no longer had any obligations to society, as society no longer recognized me. Was I obligated to be bikini ready? No. (Not that I ever was, and whatever that means even today, but now any pressure to be perfect was gone.) I was no longer obligated to be seen and not heard, no longer in anyone's shadow. Was I obligated to create meals for another? Nope. To set a table? No. Was I obligated to arrive anywhere at any time? Not anymore. This meant I could do anything, whatever I felt. I could go wherever my whims might take me.

Please know, I am not speaking of freedom from work here. I am not financially free in any way. I have debt, it has been a struggle, and I work hard. Of course 99% of us still need to earn money and maybe punch a time card. I mean this philosophically, and in regard to the rest of our day. What are our personal goals if we are free to pursue anything and everything? We can have a second career, go to school, or learn a new trade or skill.

I am suddenly limitless in my pursuits. Since no one was looking for me, I didn't have to be found. I could spend a weekend in the art studio, or on a three-hour walk in the woods with my dog. I could meditate in the bathtub, and I could eat snacks all day instead of a meal. Okay, I admit, this is probably more personal than general, more because of my often very limiting marriage rather than any big menopause revelation. Maybe it's both?

Also, I did not have to be strapped by the limits of femininity or womanhood, no longer limited by expectations of looks. Class no longer mattered either, I was a new demographic based on my age. It's commonly known as invisible. I was limitless now that society had no use or expectations of me. Excellent! There were no limits to what I could do or where I could go! Limits and restrictions of polite society were no longer holding me in, holding me up, or holding me back. If I was invisible, didn't that mean I could walk through walls too?

There was nothing to strive for now except Selfhood. I was free to be the person I wanted to be. No more molds to fit, no more hats to wear. Just my own hat, whatever I wanted it to be! I realized I had never been so free. I could wear any hat, or a scarf, a helmet, even a babushka!

The possibilities were endless. Should I go to school to become an architect to figure out saving old buildings, reusing materials, or creating sustainable communities? Should I open a bakery and coffee shop to feed the community? Should I be in the woods protecting trees? Should go study seed sovereignty under Vandana Shiva in India? Should I sail with the Sea Shepherd? Honestly, I'm still figuring it out. One thing is for certain: there are no limits, obligations or traditions holding me back.

NO COMPROMiSE

We have been taught to compromise over and over again, we've been told our accomplishments do not matter or are less important than those of our brothers, husbands, and male coworkers. We have taken the back seat forever. No more.

We are free now, today from this moment forward. It shouldn't have taken until menopause to see it and grab it, but so it goes. It does, even for the Orca. We are here now to take our place at the helm.

Now is the time for us to stand up and offer the immensity of our wisdom to the world. No more meekness. No more waiting quietly. We know the score, we know what is important. We need to teach kindness and compassion. We need to be a strong voice in the face of that which we cannot stand for any longer.

Over twenty years ago, a Yale study announced that the USA was a plutocracy, it hasn't gotten better. Today it is clear the wheels are coming off this charade of so-called capitalism. The real "welfare queens" are not single mothers, but corporations propped up by our government. The polluters, the single use plastic makers are the problem.

I am fully willing to chain myself to a tree to keep it from being cut down. I am willing to face off with any politician or corporation I disagree with. It's more than getting out into the streets in protest, though that is important. It's more than voting with our dollars, and not supporting corporations that deserve a forever boycott, though that too is important. Never underestimate how important it is!

If standing up is the end of me, so be it. I stood for something larger than myself, whether it be food, housing, equal rights for all, fighting against corporate control, control of resources, pollution, or injustice. Count me in.

IT'S THE 4TH QUARTER, IMAGINE YOUR PERFECT LiFE

Who do you want to be for the 4th quarter of your life? How do you want to present yourself?

Don't let it get you down that I am calling it the fourth quarter, the final quarter. Think about this: in retail the fourth quarter includes the Xmas season, so it goes out with a bang! In sports, the final quarter typically decides who wins the game. That makes it really exciting! The term "Grand Finale" exists for a reason!

This is a different time in our life, like no other. We have all the wisdom of our experiences behind us. Rather than thinking of death, or potentially lonely days at the nursing home, think of what you really want to do. What's the crescendo for you? What are your biggest desires? Take some time to think about it.

I have a dear friend who is kind of angry. He's your classic grumpy old man, although he's not even that old. He gets angry easily, and sometimes he makes back-handed comments. He says stuff in anger which can be a real drag, but I still like him. Obviously this person is confused by or suffering from something outside of our friendship. As the saying goes, "hurt people hurt people". And it's so true. But it's the kind of thing one has to figure out for themselves. It no longer hurts my feelings because I know it's not about me. All I can do is encourage.

It seemed like this friend was spending a lot of energy being angry for no good reason. From where I was standing, he had everything going on. He was successful in the arts, he'd worked hard, married, had kids. No matter how it had all turned out, he was in a pretty good position, at least it seemed to me. So the next time he was complaining about something, I asked this friend to imagine his perfect life. Like really imagine it.

I'm asking you to imagine yours now too. Or get ready to.

Perfect life, the idea made him sneer. I explained, "It doesn't mean you are living in a castle. Is that really a perfect life? That's a lot of maintenance, you know?" Like *really* your perfect life.

The same goes for you. What does your perfect life look like? What is your perfect life really? Now, or from today forward?

My friend makes art for a living. He has not graced the covers of 'Art In America' or 'Juxtapoz', but he does okay for himself. And, who is to say he won't still? He's got a long list of achievements. He creates the art he loves every day and people clamor for it. He's healthy and takes no medications. His longtime marriage ended, but it is amicable, and now he is free to smoke weed while sitting on his living room sofa! My grumpy friend realized he was pretty much living his perfect life. All he wanted really were a few tweaks.

"Right! So why be grumpy?" It gave him pause, and helped him see things in another perspective. Since then, he has really blossomed. He's inspired, seldom complains, and dare I say, is almost cheerful. "I'm living my perfect 13-year-old life!" He gleefully announced to me over the phone a few weeks later. Exactly!

If you are the grumpy neighbor, or the busybody on the block causing drama because you are bored and lonely, stop and ask yourself why. How did you fall into such an outlook? What is missing in your life that has blinded you from seeing all that is right all around you? You can't make people change. You can't win people over by being angry, or taking it out on them - especially if they have nothing to do with what is making you angry.

That is not to discourage you from righteous anger. Perhaps a good example of the difference between meddling and righteous anger are these two stories about my own mother:

My mother did not like the type of boys my sister was bringing home. To this point, she chased more than one off with a shovel! But maybe she overdid it trying to control my sister's life? In retrospect, perhaps those actions caused unnecessary problems in our household and for my sister in the years to come. Perhaps the boys were that bad. But rather than a shovel being the solution, maybe an honest conversation with my sister about self-worth or some therapy would have been a better option.

I want to take a moment to acknowledge that I speak of therapy a lot here, and some people have not had good therapy experiences. I have had a few who didn't seem to help very much, but you have to shop around and interview these people. I say that even if you are using free services. We are trusting them with so much; make sure they are worth it. And, a good therapist is worth their weight in gold.

Some years later, when I was living back with my mother, new tenants across the street in a brick two-flat were hosting dog fights. We could hear it. It was horrifying - the barks and cries, and worst of all, the human cheers. My mother called the police but they were afraid to act, not really equipped to deal in such matters, so she took it upon herself. My mother, wearing her nightgown and robe, flip flops, and fury, marched across the street in the night with a big flashlight and confronted a dozen or so men in a garage, calling halt to the fight in progress. She told them in no uncertain terms that this despicable behavior was not welcome here.

She could have been killed. Our house could have been targeted, maybe burned down. It would not have been unusual. Any number of terrible things could have happened. But, she was, as I wrote in her obituary, "quietly fierce", and made her point. Instead, the operation was gone the next day, and everyone on the block treated my mother forever after with admiration and total respect, and maybe a little bit of fear. What power an outraged "gray hair" can wield!

WHAT IS YOUR PERFECT LIFE?

Over the last five years I have really had to consider the question, what does my perfect life look like? When the life I thought I was having changed suddenly at age 49, I really had to ask myself as I turned 50, what does my perfect life look like now??? What do I want out of this 4th quarter?

When I thought about it, I realized my life is really amazing. Sure, I've had a hard time financially, but I've stayed positive, and I know it's not going to last forever. Yes, my divorce was shockingly contentious. Today, I feel pity for the person who needs to be so cruel after nearly a quarter century together.

I've tried to imagine someplace I would rather live, but I live in an adorable little cottage, with great neighbors. I worked hard to get this place and to hold onto it. I've been here for more than six years now, the second longest home of my adult life. I really like it here. I think even if I was a millionaire, I'd still want to live here. Sure, I see the pretty houses on the upper crust side of town. I'm okay with where I am at. I'd make a few improvements - my little cottage does need some big repairs - but this place is pretty perfect for me.

I've also reconsidered what a good relationship is. I've cultivated some amazing friendships, some of the best in my life. I have had a handful of romantic relationships these last five years, some were great and some not so great, but all romances have challenges. My goals are so different now than when I was 25. I am not looking for the same kind of relationships I was then. I'm done with the charade of forever. I'm still figuring out what I am looking for on that front. We all want to feel loved, but in what manner is individual for each of us, and even that is ever changing.

I still have a healthy sex drive and I hope to never lose that. I enjoy the intimacy of romantic partnership and the pleasure of abandon, building beautiful memories with another, and feeling mutual love and admiration. But I don't know if I'd ever want to co-habitate with a partner again. Just writing that gives me pause; this is probably a little too much information here. For me, it felt unfair to others in my romances over the last few years because my situation with my former partner was so tumultuous. I could not think of being in a serious relationship, and even officially divorced for some months now, there is no desire to change my Facebook profile to "in a relationship" status. It sounds terrifying, in fact. Not to say I don't have a great lover or two in my life, who I wish to know for the rest of my days. Love just looks different to me today. I'm seeing a therapist again, and I told him learning how to have a healthy romantic relationship is one of my goals in working with him. I'm still a work in progress.

One of my fourth quarter improvements to myself so far is that I learned to be my own best friend again, and for the first time. My inner voice is kinder, encouraging, gently offering sage advice, and most of all, forgiving. Gone is the screaming meanie my inner voice used to be. I've learned to let people like me for me. I don't need to over-perform, and I am not looking for a pat on the head. Being me, doing my best for me, is enough.

I'm not denying the gut instinct any more. It is nearly always right, and generally when I don't follow it, it's a bad time. Overall, I trust my instincts so much more today, and it feels good to have full say over my own life. I answer to no one (aside from the mortgage company and the utilities and my auto insurance, you know what I mean). I am the leader of my life, which has its challenges and benefits. And while I'm not opposed to settling down with a special someone at some point, right now I need to cut my own path.

We all have a path in life, sometimes we veer off it, and we can do that for a while, but if we don't get back on our own path we become miserable. If you are feeling down all the time, you have to ask yourself why. Do you really hate your job, your partner, your life, or have you just spent too long on a path that was not your own? What should you be doing? Were you born to do something but somehow life told you it was impractical or impossible? You can't take shouldas, couldas, or wouldas to the bank or the grave. Now is the time!

Everyone is different. My path is mine alone, not yours, and not anything you should measure yourself against. Knowing that we are all on our own path should stop any measure of comparing ourselves to others, or jealousy, or envious competition.

My sister found love and married for the first time at 50. She seems to be the happiest she has ever been. She has lived her life fully, and on her own terms. It's impressive to see her lack of conventionality has really worked out in the end. The happiest people I know are those who stood strong and did what was right for them, even in darkness, or to the chagrin of so-called society.

My perfect life is kind of what I have now. I am writing daily, making art daily, and go for long walks with my canine companion. I am enjoying friendships and even some romance with people I truly cherish, who like me for me. I don't feel like I constantly need to prove myself for acceptance, or walk on eggshells. I have faced things about myself. I am finding strength in my weaknesses, and seeing where my strengths became blinders. I have made a lot of progress learning to use meditation... And to give credit where it is due, micro-dosing mushrooms. I feel authentically me and I am at peace with that.

I marvel every day at the changes in my life! In my new line of work,

I am starting at the bottom, but I am delighted to be doing something completely new to me. It's fun and frustrating, and there is so much to learn and I am so green. It came into my life exactly when I needed it and out of nowhere. It is sometimes hard, and it can be sweaty, but I like that too. I'm learning useful new skills every day, and while it might not be my life's goal, it is serving me at the moment in many ways. I'm enjoying the change of pace and the education, but also the flexibility of the work. And, I don't feel morally opposed to what we create and produce. I will never take a job I don't believe in.

If this fourth quarter is more of that - more resolving my trauma and issues, more finding my way on my path without compromise and with a measure of success, at least enough to maintain. That seems pretty good. If I can do more even better. I am keeping my heart and my mind open.

When I think of my perfect life, I feel like I am actually pretty close. That doesn't mean I don't sometimes feel despair. It is part of the human condition. We are spiritual beings. Beings of light and waveform. We are not solids but an ever-changing mass of cells and molecules and spirit, of which science still knows painfully little. I count myself lucky; I have a devoted dog and an amazing turtle in my life. I have wonderful neighbors, including countless birds and squirrels. I love my shabby little cottage and my wild yard. Let's call it rustic. I am proud of the work I have done in life, and I have taken the time to create a clear vision of where I am going. I have learned from my failures, and I can finally see my successes. Best of all, I am excited to wake up every single morning.

A while back I was listening to the radio, I listen to local community radio stations mostly; currently it is KBOO. The show was an arts show of some sort and they were interviewing the curator of a Judy Chicago art exhibit that was installed locally for a limited time at the Jewish History Museum. The way the curator spoke of Judy Chicago was enthralling, in a way in which artists seldom can, if ever, speak of themselves. Artists, myself included, can be pretty obtuse and inarticulate when speaking about their own work. Until hearing this interview I knew very little about her, aside from she was a successful living female artist.

The curator spoke of Judy Chicago having an idea for a photo study using colored smoke. Her solution was to attend pyrotechnic training school and get certified in the field. A year or more of study later, she mixed her own chemicals and made exactly the effects she envisioned for this particular study in her art. She went to depths to make these photos exactly what she wanted them to be. This was so refreshing to hear. She didn't hire an expert; she became an expert! I made sure to go see the exhibit while it was up. It was a small but potent collection of a life lived with conviction and cause. That seemed like a great measure of success.

I am not suggesting we measure ourselves by Judy Chicago. I am suggesting we could be inspired by her thirst for knowledge, her conviction, and her cause. I think we all have that. What are you thirsting to know about? I have some secret desires; I'd hate to die before I get to pursue a few of them. Do you know what I mean?

I played the clarinet in the school band from third through sixth grade. I would love to pick that back up, and maybe learn guitar. I know that probably sounds silly, but so what? I'm free.

A LiTTLE SELF-CARE INTERLUDE...

Sometimes the best thing we can do is just live in the moment. If you find yourself feeling upset, maybe stop for a moment and catch your breath. Slow your breathing, slow and lengthen your inhales and exhales for a minute or two. Step away from the thoughts into the moment. Focusing on our breath and re-centering ourselves takes less than a minute to do. Look around at where you are. What beauty can you find in this moment? What lesson can you learn or teach?

With all that is going on in the world, and all we are dealing with personally, and as light as I'm trying to be here, essentially what I am speaking of is death. Our death, and that is a heavy thing to think about.

I understand. I too get overwhelmed at the notion of dying. At the idea of reaching my end. But, I feel great right now, so I can't get bogged down by it. I can accept it. I can use it to propel myself forward, but I will not live like the condemned.

I read recently that hearing birds sing has a grounding effect similar to walking barefoot on the ground, - grass, sand, moss, or dirt. Obviously not asphalt. Asphalt is one of the plagues of our modern world; asphalt will be remembered as a shameful part of our history someday. Walk barefoot on the ground, sit or stand on a patch of ground for twenty minutes a day, it is healing. Listen to the birds.

Meditation, too, has helped me so very much. People have all kinds of ideas what that means. I sure did. Today, I like to meditate just lying in bed, or in the bathtub. I'll put some candles around the tub and soak in epsom salt and scenty stuff. Maybe I'll find a nice guided meditation online, or listen to music and create my own experience.

There's a little hill in my backyard. Back in the day, it's where the people who lived here buried their trash. I like to sit outside on this little hill and meditate sometimes, weather permitting. I have had some interesting experiences, communions with my yard wildlife. A cat passing by, not seeing me until I opened my eyes. Once I posed a question, opened my eyes, and looked up just as a bald eagle flew above me heading east about 20 feet in the air!

Meditation is as simple as breathing. As thoughts come through I try to merely observe them and let them pass. If we open to our higher self, and listen for answers to our real questions or inspirations, they will come.

Yoga too can help so much. Sometimes I just stand in 'downward dog' or sit in 'extended child's pose' for five or so minutes to let go of something that is bothering me, known or just felt.

When I was married, my husband fell ill with what turned out to be gout. We went to the emergency room and the doctor who treated him, an older woman with a flat top haircut, said emphatically, "Go for walks in nature! As soon as you are able, start walking in nature, among the trees. It is really healing. It is scientifically proven to be healing". She was so right. When I think about it, even in my youth, if I went and spent time in the forest, I felt right.

Self-care is no joke, these are heavy topics. Breathe, and know you are loved.

FOR THE FOURTH QUARTER PLANNiNG iS iMPORTANT

The fourth quarter of a year ends with big holidays and parties, fun, and obligation. You are remembered for the gifts bestowed. It's the same with this fourth quarter in life: it's the big one! Get organized, tell the family stories that need to be passed down, tell the history of the heirlooms. Give stuff away to people who you want to have it now and lighten your load. What are you giving? Are you ready to plan this?

I think by now I have probably suggested making some kind of list. Maybe it's time to start putting pen or pencil to paper? Let's make it official.

This is a manifesto, not a workbook. Your work book is yours for the making or not. Get a cheap spiral notebook or some fancy Red & Black pad, it's up to you. Find a few good pens or pencils that feel good in your hand and on the paper.

I'm going to refer to the great catalyst for creativity and clarity here, Julia Cameron, and her remarkable book 'The Artist's Way'. One part of her method for working through creative blocks, and charting our creative path in general, is an exercise she calls "The Morning Pages", and her specific encouragement made all the difference for me. The book was gifted to me a few years back, and I am forever thankful for it!

In the book, the author speaks of taking a few minutes every morning to write a couple pages, a total stream of consciousness practice to see what comes up. With this practice she makes two great suggestions. First, not to read any of it back for a few weeks. That freedom really helped me. Second, she said initially the stream of consciousness may be a lot of complaining and not to let it hinder the continuation of the practice. Reading that helped me work through it and not beat myself up for being negative. These were important for me to note, and probably made all the difference between the success or failure of staying committed to it. She was right, it leveled out after a few weeks and the real accomplishment came through!

I took up journaling right after my marriage ended to help heal, but this was different. It was writing for clarity. It took me a while to differentiate what was for the journal and what was for the morning pages. I finally figured out a system that worked for me. My journal is private, whereas the morning writings often became essays that I might want to share. Some of them are here within these very pages!

In another book on writing, 'Writing Down The Bones', author Nancy Goldberg suggests we often hold on to fancy notebooks waiting for something important to write in them and then never write, so she swore by cheap spiral notepads. There is a strange difference in writing in a journal with a fancy cover and writing in a $2 notepad. At least for me, I found this to be true. A small stack of beautiful journals, one with handmade paper even, currently sit blank in my drawer. I will change that!

You will have to decide what works for you, I am sharing this exercise with you. Make a commitment to try to write daily in a notebook, fancy or plain (and why not go fancy, it's the fourth quarter after all!) I can't use those fancy journals when I'm dead.

If you have trouble starting, why don't you take the first page or pages to write your obituary if you were to die today?

Wait, did I just say write your obituary? Yep, I did. Write that obituary down.

WRiTE YOUR OBiTUARY

If you are struggling to figure out what is still on your list in this life, perhaps a better way to start is by looking back at your life first and seeing where you have been. So, why not write your obituary?

Take a good long look at your life so far.

What are the highlights? Are they the moments you thought they'd be?

If we can take an honest look at our lives, we can more easily identify what will be fulfilling for us in this final quarter?

If your obituary was written today, what would be on there?

Just write it down. Don't over think it. Put down anything, no matter how trivial, that comes to mind, just a list to start. This includes 4H ribbons, student or employee of the month awards, that time you won money or appeared on 'Family Feud'. All of your various achievements, your family members who are surviving you. All of it, whatever you got.

I wrote my mother's obituary, which took me a week. Much of the time was me lying in bed, yelling at myself in my head that I couldn't do it. But in my defense, my mother had just died. In the end, it finally just flowed out in one long stream. I recalled things from her life the best I could, from my own memories, and memories of her stories about her youth. I didn't do her justice, but how can you? How do we do anyone's life justice in a few sorrow filled paragraphs? Everyone is a book.

Come to think of it, I wrote my father's obituary too. These are difficult things.

From a practicality standpoint, having an obituary at the ready that can be added to with every new achievement is not a bad idea. Call me morbid; so what? Bonus side effects include taking pressure off loved ones while they are mourning us to construct an obituary, and we control the narrative. The reason I suggest writing one is to take a look at all we have accomplished in our lives. At this point, we have achieved more than we probably realized. We also may discover themes in our lives we'd overlooked before and perhaps there is something calling to us for this fourth quarter plan.

Last year, while spring cleaning around the house, I decided to go through some drawers in the desk in my bedroom. I was surprised to run across ribbons from a county fair. I'd placed with a few things I'd baked, including the Championship ribbon for the Quick-breads category! It was for lavender vanilla scones I'd invented just for the fair. I received a beautiful purple ribbon proclaiming my achievement and $3. It was the best $3 I ever won!

I'd forgotten all about it. Now I remembered standing in line at the fairgrounds waiting to enter, in mild disbelief that county fairs existed, and you could win ribbons! And I did win a ribbon, three in fact! My husband won some ribbons too for his art. We were elated, like little kids full of glee!

We'd only learned about it a few weeks earlier at Granny Patty's Feed Store, in beautiful Knappa Oregon. We'd stopped there to check out some plants and look around one day. On the counter was a stack of brochures with all the categories one could enter at the upcoming county fair, pages and pages of code numbers. It was all very mysterious. Granny Patty must have noticed my bewildered look and explained. She said you could enter for any of the categories listed and be judged, and maybe win a ribbon. There was everything from string art to canned jam! How fun it was to enter a county fair! As a kid, I would not have been able to fathom such a thing! A county fair sounded like something from a fairytale to my urban upbringing.

I enjoyed the forgotten memory and hung the ribbon from a candle holder on my wall outside my kitchen door to remind myself that even seemingly small achievements are important. It's on my wall still today. Ironically, only one person has ever inquired what it was and if it was real. They almost didn't believe me when I said that indeed it was real and I had won it with scones! Seems like a lifetime ago.

You probably have a bunch of stuff like that -- high score bowling, maybe performing or speaking, an article in the newspaper, the trip of a lifetime, career goals fulfilled. Noting our accomplishments is important.

It made me think of all the lifetimes I have lived: from my first job to living on my own, to living in tiny Ely Minnesota, to living in an old broken down RV on a beach in the Pacific Northwest. The various lifetimes of my youth, as a wife, and now this new chapter I have embarked upon. These are my experiences.

You undoubtedly have your own achievements (likely more and greater achievements than mine, certainly different). While some may seem similar, like marriage, jobs, and travel, they are still different. My visit to the Grand Canyon and your visit to the Grand Canyon are completely different, even if some of our pictures do look the same.

Who are the family and friends you will want to mention? Make a list of them too.

Make a list of all the schooling or career milestones you have achieved.

Are there organizations you support or are part of? Have you volunteered? Ever won a trophy or a ribbon for anything? Put it down on your list.

Start by simply making this list of your achievements. As the list of achievements fills out, perhaps you will start to see themes in your life. Then, when you make it chronological, you will see the twists and turns life took. It's fun if you let it be. It doesn't have to be so macabre.

My county fair ribbon discovery brought back something I'd completely forgotten about. As your list obituary fills out, you will undoubtedly be surprised at yourself!

We are in this body only once, and then we go back to stardust and energy. Looking back over our lives is important. Not to turn to salt, not in a regret-filled longing for the past, but in a celebration! It is also a personal investigation to see what brought us real joy over these decades. Take stock of all you have done, and how far you have come. It should help you appreciate yourself more, and get clues on what is next.

IMMORTALITY

Immortality exists well within the world where we dwell. You could certainly achieve it; I could too. Immortality is about what we leave behind. Think of Shakespeare. Even if his work is no longer required reading for today's schoolchildren, it was certainly a reading requirement in my day, and is still very much alive in popular culture, everyone has heard of Romeo and Juliet.

Songwriters and performers such as Johnny Cash, David Bowie, and Sister Rosetta Tharpe live on. Though they are no longer among us, they still exist in every day of our lives, as vital and physical as ever for those who listen to their music, or those who perform their music today. They create the soundtrack of our lives still, and potentially for decades to come! Just as the words of authors and poets live on, and actors and directors live on forever in their films.

The words of Oscar Wilde, Albert Camus, and Charles Bukowski are affecting us every day, even those who have never read a word of their work. Their influence on society is impacting the lives of people who may never know their name. A great example of this is Louis Sullivan, the 19th century architect who essentially created the "Chicago School" of Architecture. He created majesty; he trained Frank Lloyd Wright. His words "Form follows function", though horrifically reinterpreted today are still alive even to those who have never heard Sullivan's name. Did Mary Shelley know that the Frankenstein she created during a summer getaway would so profoundly affect us all still today? Did she even intend its deep sociological and psychological implications?

Immortality does not require we write a bestseller or win an Oscar. Rather, we can be immortal in many so different ways. Beyond the nonsense of celebrity, our teachers live on and our mentors, and anyone who made an impact on us long after they are gone, and everytime we have shared those stories or lessons with others. Is that not immortality? People become immortal from every walk of life, from Norma Ray to Jane Addams to Sojourner Truth to Sacajawea. We step above, when we carry on, when we do what is right rather than maintaining the status quo, when we walk on our own path, then we can become exceptional - and even immortal!

Recently, a woman sat on my tattered sofa and told me how she felt bad for her parents' success. They had earned much in life and created some level of wealth, which they planned to pass on to her. She was sheepish about this with an awkward guilt I've seen before on people who have won in life's lottery through inheritance or other good fortune. Perhaps it is because I am so obviously of modest means, but I am happy for everyone's good fortune.

"I told them I don't want the money and they should just donate it", she told me.

"Why?" I questioned. "Do you think a charity with all its overhead and administrative costs could spend your parent's money better than you? You know them, you know what would make them proud."

She looked at me puzzled; this was maybe not the reaction she expected. I told her she was missing an opportunity to offer immortality to her parents and/or herself. I explained how, a few years back, I found myself attending the scholarship award presentation for a small town high school, and that I was moved to tears as young people were presented with scholarships for college. Well over a hundred scholarships were presented, many recipients receiving more than one, and each a notch toward building their future. They will never forget that moment and the generosity they received. The community where this happened was not a rich community, and with more than half of America's school children living in poverty, those scholarships potentially meant the difference between a successful future or a life of struggle. They were given a great alternative to working the low wage, tourism-based jobs that the area offered.

I told the woman how students were given scholarships in the name of small businesses, local individuals, and a variety of organizations. Even the local motorcycle club gave $1200 to a student planning to study mechanics. There were scholarships given by families in the name of a lost child, or a deceased parent who was a teacher. A sports coach from the 1950s was kept alive as the namesake of a scholarship for a student who had participated in sports and planned to continue it in college. One family presenting their scholarship spoke of how much they loved getting to know the students. One of the daughters choked up at the podium telling how it had been so hard to choose this year, so the family decided to offer two scholarships because two of the applicants (and it being a small, fairly rural high school, there may have been only two) were both so deserving.

"Imagine" I said to my guest, "that could be you. You could create a scholarship with that inheritance and give money every year to someone based on parameters that matter to you and your parents - maybe someone from this neighborhood who wants to be an engineer, or study physics, or another young Asian woman who doesn't have the successful parents you do."

"You could use that money to maintain a park in perpetuity, to build some kind of housing for people, fund a program of some sort. You can decide!"

Even if this small volume is all I ever do before I die, and even if it brings me no acknowledgment and only three people ever read it, perhaps some words within it might affect some other person who might affect the world in some wonderful way. Or perhaps some little something I leave to one of my nieces, or to a friend, will change their lives in some way that will cause them to make a difference.

Certainly, Henrietta Lacks had no idea the impact her life would have on our world when her cancer cells were harvested by doctors. I get that might not be the immortality you want, but I'd rather be Henrietta Lacks than Dorothea Puente, who was convicted as a serial killer. No offense to Dorothea, who was always kind to me, but being infamous is maybe something else. While Dorothea, like Typhoid Mary and certainly many others, received a bum rap in a lot of ways, that's not the notoriety I am looking for.

Immortality is a funny thing. We can be remembered for our powerful foresight, or we can be forgotten for its lack. We can be immortal for being the loser that drank and/or gambled away the family's fortune.

We will all be an old photo someday. What will they say about you?

MAKE YOUR WiLL, BUT MAKE YOUR WILL

I wrote my will yesterday. I was having a bit of a low week, I guess. Nothing official, just a preliminary list of things I wish to land in the hands of certain people. I used to make a will every time I went on a trip. Just hand written and left on the counter somewhere in the event of doom.

It needs to be done, no doubt. But just writing it out made me take things into perspective. I was reminded that my days are numbered. Ours all are.

Then today, as I came across that list in my notepad, I turned the page and began to write My Will.

Realizing my folly on the first list, I began to write what was vastly more important than where my stuff goes when I'm gone: rather, what is my will in this final act? What do I wish to still accomplish and achieve?

We cannot go back to redo stuff that happened, but we can try to resolve our mistakes and regrets. We can fix many of our errors. We can put an end to our generational trauma. We can learn things we always dreamed of but never had the time, like self-care, better habits, or calligraphy.

Sure, make a will, but then, make Your Will. Write it down, be thoughtful about it. Where is your will pulling you?

Stream of consciousness writing or automatic writing can be a good exercise for this. Sit down and write everything you ever hoped to accomplish in life. From there, see what stands out. What has merit to you and your being?

Now create Your Will. It needs to be yours and yours alone, not based on obligations, the approval of others, or what you think is appropriate. Please be inappropriate! Be all over the place!

Consider your emotional will, your ambitions, your interests, your wildest dreams. Use all of it, fill pages and pages, and then take the items that really matter and create Your Will.

Once you have Your Will identified and listed, begin pursuing those goals.

We are not guaranteed tomorrow, so work hard and work fast.

Even if your will is to take it easy and slow your pace, work at it. Cultivate the past-times you fantasize about. Even if you've done it all, there has to be something more you dream of.

It's a guarantee that someone could use your help, your knowledge and wisdom, or just a hand held. Maybe there's an old friend you want to look up, or a debt you need to pay. Now is that time; do not delay!

PREP TALK PEP TALK - WHAT IS YOUR WILL?

We need to be ready for our physical mortality in the plane of existence. Who knows if the lights just go out or if something amazing lights up? Not me, and I'm not worried about it. I'm living in the here and now.

We need to think well and prepare for the just and proper uses of the money, works and writing, jewelry, and whatever artifacts we leave behind. Does your family know about the plate that came overseas in the meager possessions of a long departed ancestor? Do they know the golden wisdom in your journals? Are they aware of the silver coins hidden in the attic that could change your family's lives, maybe even put someone through college?

Which brings us to this next important part, have you made your will? And, have you made Your Will? Sure these sound the same but they are totally different.

First, your will. There is a good chance that at this point in life, you may already have this done. You and your partner, or on your own, or at the urging of your children, have sat with an attorney and created a will. Or you are planning to at some point in the near future. I've just got to say here, we are in menopause, we have won the lottery of life for some 20,000 days, but we won't always be so lucky. Get your stuff in order! I am saying this as someone with nothing in order. But hopefully writing these words will make me change it soon.

Who gets the antique dining table and who gets the jewelry? Where your 401k money goes is important too, but there are plenty of things in your home and life that you may have overlooked because they are precious, but not particularly valuable. Look with new eyes at the things in your life that you wish to pass on and to whom, and create some sort of addendum.

Beyond the monetary stuff, there is so much more! Do you have it down if your friend Suzy gets your rock collection and your neighbor gets your cookbooks? There's a lot more than you think probably. Make sure your true wishes are known. Or give it to them now and get it off your plate.

A will is something we are all well aware of and need to consider now to ensure things go where we want them to, that our descendants know the true valuables in our lives and our homes, and so we can hopefully avoid any ugliness with our kin while they are in the depths of grief at our passing.

Society tells us, even those of us with the meagerest of means, that a will is vital in the event of our inevitable passing. Equally as important, but sadly something most of us never consider is that we should also take time to make Our Will - a list of items, goals, etcetera that we wish to accomplish before we go into that good night.

Those of us with modest means can create a will, get two friends to sign as witnesses, and head over to your local credit union or UPS store or wherever and get it notarized. Maybe mail a copy to one or two people you trust. That ought to be enough.

You may have a "bucket list" written or in your head, and Your Will is that for sure, but it is also so much more. What are your wishes for your loved ones? Do they know? Are there fences that need mending? Is there unfinished business you have here or there? Do you owe your son or daughter an apology for some narrow minded thinking? Do you owe someone some harsh words? Have you been keeping a secret and it's eating away inside you? Make it happen now.

What are your goals and dreams for this part of your life? If you haven't thought about it, which is common in this live fast, die young world of America. Reaching middle age is often not planned for, nor thought of with much regard. "Old" was usually some abstract idea that we don't actually fit as we get here. Let us use this time! What is yet to achieve?

Beyond the nuts and bolts, older age isn't what it was 50 years ago. There is no gold watch, no pension, no retirement freedom at 55. If you are one of the lucky ones with a pension, or a lucky strike, then you have even more reason to plan. What do you want 50 and up to look like? Give it some thought, and start writing down your ideas. Jot them down for a week or two and then go back and refine them.

Create a final list of goals and dreams, a final list of desired achievements. What do you WILL for yourself at this point in life - without limitations and constraints. Now is that time to decide!

DEATH COMES FOR US ALL

"If I ever die..." Ever hear this phrase? I heard it a lot as a kid and a teenager. Macabre as I was, I would always correct, "When you die, you mean?"

I can only speak for America, but here we have a weird fear of death. The very fact we are alive at this moment means we are going to die. It's how it goes, it's the cycle of life. Time passes, things change, we die.

There is no use in fearing the reaper. Death is coming. Every day that we wake up, we are winning the lottery so many others did not. Rather than worrying and fearing death, we ought to be loving every moment we have! I, personally, do not have time for commercials, traffic jams, or long lines. I want to live! Sure, I'll accept a certain amount of nonsense. There's no avoiding traffic sometimes, but does that kind of grind really benefit society, or us as individuals? It doesn't seem like it.

America's fear of death as a culture is a weird thing. We cannot seem to embrace it the way our friends south of the border and many other cultures do. The Day of the Dead in Mexico, aside from celebrating ancestors and loved ones passed, also allows for skeletal and skull dress up, an acceptance that our bodies are temporary vessels.

The one place in America that has a good understanding of death is New Orleans, but they are an ancient city, far older than America. A local historian explained to me once how that city was a center of trade long before Columbus showed up. It was a place where Native Americans and South Americans, and every manner of islander came to exchange goods. Ancient peoples have traversed this planet for thousands of years, from the Vikings to the ancient Chinese. Modern history attempts to hide these facts, but that is another story for another day.

The point of bringing up New Orleans is their Jazz Funeral. The beauty and honor of the jazz funeral is an acceptance that death is part of the ride. They are sad at the beginning, then everyone is dancing at the end. Life goes on. The above ground cemeteries there, though born from necessity, offer another reminder far deeper, and with greater honor than the grassy cemeteries elsewhere. An inescapable reminder of mortality in brick and mortar! Nowhere else in America is the philosophy of "Eat, drink, and be merry for tomorrow we die" more in your face and accepted than in that ancient city on the Gulf.

Yeah, death is coming for you and it is coming for me. What are we going to do about it? Instead of standing still in worry and dread, we must push forward to accomplish all we can, do to fulfill ourselves in the tiny space of time that is our life in this body.

As the iconic author, Jack London, so profoundly surmises, "I would rather be ashes than dust! I would rather that my spark should burn out in a brilliant blaze than it should be stifled by dry-rot. I would rather be a superb meteor, every atom of me in magnificent glow, than a sleepy and permanent planet. The proper function of man is to live, not to exist. I shall not waste my days in trying to prolong them. I shall use my time." There is really no better way to say it.

So what are you stressing about pointless bullshit for? We all have a purpose to fulfill. Maybe it's something big, I feel like this little project I am creating is bigger than me, but maybe it's small. Maybe our true purpose is just to heal ourselves.

Science is proving more every day that we are all connected. What Edgar Cayce called the "one mind" way back when. That means when humans on the other side of the world are suffering, we feel it somewhere in our bodies too. Therefore, if we are able to stop our own suffering, to release our own trauma and fear, then maybe that helps heal everyone, including the planet. Maybe healing ourselves could stop wars on the other side of the world?

Why do we allow things to go so wrong? We were born into a paradise, but all we think about is fighting. Each of us is here for a reason. What is that reason? And what are we as orca pod leaders going to do? Doesn't matter who "they" say is in power. We are in power. Taking a nod from our Orca brethren, we are taking the lead. From here on out, nothing will be same. Let us use our time.

BEYOND DEATH

There is something that needs to be addressed, and I'll be as brief as possible on it because it is hard to think about. What if we are left in that state between life and death for a long period of time? I'm talking about being incapacitated, losing our faculties, or a long and painful illness. What do we do then?

When my father had a stroke he was paralyzed on his left side. The doctors said he would never walk again. I learned an important lesson. People plan for their death, but no one plans for being incapacitated. An envelope in his address book said, "Open in the event of my death". Inside it he said who got the deer plates and statues he'd collected, and instructed the reader to "clean out the liquor cabinet". There was nothing for "Open in the event I am paralyzed". He was lucky, he worked hard in physical therapy and he got his mobility back. After a while he didn't even use a cane. But, everyone is not so lucky. What if that happens to you?

If you need to check out, have you prepared? Don't wait until you are incapable of making that decision. I am not promoting suicide here at all, but it seems unfair that we can euthanize our trusted furry companion to end their suffering, but we cannot for our catatonic or otherwise suffering parent or partner. The state I live in allows for assisted suicide for terminally ill people, but there are a lot of steps and procedures to allow for it. I don't know what is morally right; kindness and compassion looks different in some situations. Historically, in some eastern European cultures, and certainly beyond, there would be a member of the community who served to end other's suffering with a blow from a specially designed hammer. This person, usually a woman, was revered for this service. It is a daunting task, but was done in compassion to end suffering in the days before a morphine drip.

It's heavy stuff we have to think about. I bring it up to say consider this! Prepare for anything, and have contingency plans for yourself to stay vital in these times. How do you want to go out? Some things are bigger than us. Maybe at some point we use our decrepit bodies to lie down for something big. Maybe we all go to war torn places, where people are treated intolerably, or the planet is being raped, and we stand up by laying our bodies down on the front lines? If people in wheelchairs can climb Mt. Everest, we can do something no matter what state we are in to help make a difference. We do not have to fade out in front of the TV at the nursing home. Let's run, walk, or crawl to that final finish line!

GRiEF iS EXHAUSTiNG

Grief is one of those things that there's no getting out of. Like death, grief keeps us on an even playing field. If we love, we will grieve.

You are gonna grieve in this life. We all are. I have. I've lost both my parents, and a long marriage ended. I've lost friends, so many friends! I've suffered the loss of a handful of dearly loved canine companions, and any number of other creatures I loved and said goodbye to: various feral cats, squirrels, birds, toads, a hermit crab. I've witnessed tragedy. I've had to leave places I thought would always be part of my life. I lost everything I owned in a fire at 21, and then again in a storage disaster twenty years later. One might say I have experienced life to the fullest.

We all have our scars. There's no way you got here without grief. And there is bound to be more.

Grief is exhausting. It weighs heavy, and it takes up a lot of energy. You are going to need extra rest, probably for a good span of time. Months maybe. Grief is a long marathon, it's a slow process.

When someone dies, people traditionally bring over food. There's a reason for that. It's because grief is a debilitating experience. I believe the practice in Jewish culture of sitting Shiva is a beautiful ritual and an honoring of not just the deceased, but the mourners too.

In America, we barely get bereavement time if someone close to us dies, and there's no time off for "my life just imploded situations" like divorce, or emotional trauma from an accident, or a disaster. The bills don't stop! If your house and everything you held dear washed away tomorrow, the mortgage and bills keep coming! Hopefully, someday soon grief will be treated with gentler hands so people can take the time they need to rest, mourn and cope. It's so weird: in modern America, most people are lucky to get three days of bereavement time off their jobs if their partner dies, or their parent, or god forbid, their kid. Three days.

Years ago I was told a story about grief by Larkin Stentz. He's a colorful character I had the pleasure of working with when I volunteered at his organic farm way back around 2009 and 2010, on the Long Beach Peninsula along the southern coast of Washington state. He bought the house and land with his wife years earlier with the dream of fully sustainable living, and providing organic food to the community. They did a CSA (that's "Community Supported Agriculture"), and had a small farm store. His wife became ill and had passed away sometime before I met him, but his heartbreak was still evident, and her presence still felt around the place.

When my father passed away, Larkin shared the story a hospice nurse told him when his wife was dying. It really helped me out, and I have shared it with others in grief. It goes something like this:

"Grief is like a book. When we first experience our loss, we cannot put the book down. It keeps us from being able to do anything, because we have to carry it all the time. As time goes on we are able to put the book down for short periods of time to get things done, but we have to keep picking up the book. Then we can put it down more and more, but the book is right there on the table and we are looking at it all the time. Finally, we can put the book on the shelf and it's there. We've filled more of our life around it and we carry on, but sometimes still, that book comes flying off the shelf and strikes you in the forehead."

There's my best paraphrasing. I'm sure not as eloquent as Larkin's original telling. I have told this little tale to many people struggling to combat grief in some mandated period of time. Grief takes it's time. I don't think I really felt like myself for a year after my father died, I think it was the same with my mother, maybe even longer.

It's really important to accept and feel the grief. The best way to process it is straight through. I made the mistake of throwing myself into my work when my beloved Pitbull Roxanne passed away. She was the first canine of my adult life. She came to live with me just before I turned 20, and was with me through thick and thin until I was 32 or 33. We had been through so much together. I needed to grieve my friend, but instead I threw myself into work. A year later, I still felt I had not mourned her.

There are many kinds of grief. Grief for what was, and what never was. There's the grief of diminishing. Losing an ability we took for granted, like being able to walk, or having two arms, or two kidneys, or life before an oxygen tank was a permanent companion. Anyone who's watched a parent fade from dementia knows grief can be a long slow ride.

Relationships are entities, and when they end that is another time of grief, no matter how amicable the end is. There is a sorrow of ending, of course, for all the dreams and plans unfulfilled. It is a death of that entity. It took a long time to grieve when my own marriage ended. I am so thankful I found yoga and meditation and small mushroom doses to help process, because I had to maintain a full-time job through it all with only a few days off until the pandemic began fourteen months later.

Until recently, if I was asked to recall something about the first six months or so after the end of my marriage, I'd often start losing my train of thought, or go off on weird tangents of stress, but it has gotten much better since the official end finally came about six months ago. My stress level is way down after four years of trying to get divorced (but who's counting). My life is full and rich, filled with good people, vibrance, and beauty -- and I never thought I would ever feel that way. So there is great progress, but it took time.

Grief isn't easy, but we are not alone in this. We are all together with it. Reach out to others if you need a hand. Lean on friends, take your time, see a therapist, and definitely practice self-care, whatever that means to you. If you know someone grieving, be there for them. Be a friend, or a good neighbor. Be a human being. We are all in this together. Are there support groups for grief in communities? If not, maybe there should be.

Years ago, I worked for a company that allowed us to donate our own personal time off to a fellow co-worker if they were sick with cancer or something. It's a nice concept; since the company wasn't going to help, they would let us. We don't need some company to give us such a policy. What if we put together small grief teams to help our fellow human beings? There's a simple improvement that could change lives, with little effort and a shareable online calendar. I remember people bringing casseroles and and sandwiches and stuffed green peppers when my grandparents died.

Grief has its beauty too. We only grieve that which we love. To know love, how wonderful a thing! If we know much love and therefore great swells of grief, how lucky we are!

ONLY AS STRONG AS THE WEAKEST DECKHAND

Years ago, I lived in a small fishing town on the Oregon and Washington border, and had the great good fortune to count a few real commercial fishermen among my friends. One in particular, Dave Densmore, who is also a great poet, was full of wisdom he was not afraid to share. One day he said that the crew of a fishing boat was "only as strong as it's weakest deckhand".

This concept gave me pause when he said it, and I have come back to it again and again over the years in various situations. More recently, I heard Earl Nightingale say something similar in his profound 1956 recording of 'The Strangest Secret'. He said the military formation can only move as fast as the slowest vehicle. I prefer the deckhand version, so I'll stick with that.

Anyway, how does this relate to menopause? Well, really, it relates to all of life. We are not the same, some of us are faster or stronger than others, and some of us are more deliberate in our thinking. Some of us are slow and methodical. Who is right? All of us.

What a terrible doomed world we would be in if we were all expected to be the same, to run as fast as each other, to be as quick witted, to all be able to lift 400 pounds. Sure, I fantasize about doing complex math problems, and being a great chess player, and traveling to tropical places. None of those are me though. I can't manage my checkbook, and I suck at chess, but

I am compassionate and empathetic like no other, to a fault sometimes. I can bake a cookie without conscious thought, though I'm not the greatest cookie baker ever, I'm pretty good. I've been told I am upbeat. I am a natural observer and an excellent problem solver. We all have our charms. I'll say that again: we all have our charms.

At this point in life, we have seen a lot of things, met a lot of people, and done plenty of different stuff. No two of us have seen the same things, met all the same people, or done the same stuff. Sure there is overlap, but not identical - even if we are conjoined twins our experiences are in some way different. We are all looking out our own eyes.

Getting back to the deckhand analogy: there are the skiff drivers and the cooks, the net mender and the skipper. Each is dependent on the others to survive and to flourish. A boat of all cooks or all skippers isn't gonna work. The fishing boat's crew with their varied skills and roles, their diversity of knowledge and experience is not only beautiful to see in action; it is vital for their success and survival. It is the same for the continuation of mankind. We are not all skiff drivers. We are not all skippers or cooks. We each have our special purpose, and not just me and you, but all those around us too.

If we took to heart that we are only as strong as our weakest deckhand and thought of it globally, how does that work out? If we are all each other's deckhands, how fast can we go? How far can we reach when our fellow man is dodging bombs somewhere, or being forced to do dangerous labor for terrible pay? We as a species cannot move up to enlightenment until we stop blasting one another away for wars of belief, resources, or turf.

To hear the fishermen tell it so eloquently, a good crew moves in a rhythm, each doing their job and watching each other's backs. It's a smooth flow. A bad crew is a bad summer The fish will feel it and stay away, mistakes are made, foolishness may erupt. A bad seed is mercilessly left on the dock rather than jeopardize the season for the team. The skipper or captain must see and resolve the problems in a crew that cannot grow cohesive. Their lives depend on it.

And not to call anyone a Bad Seed, but sometimes our electromagnetics repel rather than attract. Then, we need to move elsewhere and find our place. I'm not pushing some elitist philosophy. I'm suggesting if we all do what we are good at instead of whatever we are coaxed into by circumstance, then we'd find where we fit, where we offer what is needed to the world. We can find where harmony can grow with those around us.

Marshall Field was born to set the standard of a quality merchant. He would be horrified by what retail shopping is today and the poor quality goods of our world. Mark Twain brought us what he was born to do, in words. Malcolm X led because he was called to lead. I've met people who were born to work with plants and growing things, or to educate children, or to create incredible food, and they are doing it.

If we all work together it is a dance of life, of moving forward to a new place in the world. Each of us has a role in it.

FOR THE MEN iN OUR LiVES: CHANGiNG FROM THE WARRiOR TO THE SHAMAN, WiSE MAN, OR CHiEF

If you have a man or men in your life, whether they be brother, lover, partner, or friend, help them along to see the merits of the next chapter in their lives. No doubt, women can be provider, farmer, shaman, or chieftain. We can be all of it. But we need to consider our counterparts. Even if you are a militant lesbian, we all owe it to the future to help our male counterparts along on this journey. It is hard for them too, and they do not have menopause to assist as rite of passage. They are just suddenly not the man they were. Men's midlife crises can be violent or dangerous to those around them. Sadly, it's often merely in their perception of themselves and not even reality -- they fall for marketing too! Symptoms include over splurging, casting aside a long devoted partner, acting the fool or like a reckless teenager, even losing their minds.

In my own marriage, all the big stuff, solving the hard times, fixing the major mistakes or unforeseen disasters always fell on my shoulders. My partner was a lousy provider. He never got the tools he needed growing up, and the many tricks of his ego kept him stalled. I've seen better men than him lose their minds over the change from warrior to wise man. They want to continue to fight, but they are no longer possessing of battle strength. Their power has shifted. It must shift. They are becoming something else at this point, something equally valuable, but so often they fail to see it. While different than our own foolish actions, men often fall into a whole host of their own bizarre behaviors to try to avoid realizing their mortality. But there is no cheating time or death.

Perhaps you are feeling indignant for such a chapter to be in this book of all books. But I assure you, it is most vital for us here to understand. Serve and protect is the motto, not of our militarized police bullies, but the duty of all women everywhere. No community exists without us. Even the male dominated secret societies like the masons or the elks need the guidance of we women to survive and thrive. We are the backbone. Without our potato salad and intuitive advice, those organizations would have likely faltered long ago.

It is a fact: behind every great man is a great woman. We lend our strength and a great deal of our time to the men, the children, and the infirm. You live alone you say? Never married? Supported yourself? Yeah, well, you let some man off the hook in doing so. Even if only a theoretical man. We cannot hate others for our subjugation, and we cannot be free if we turn and subjugate them as revenge or our right. My rise does not mean others need to be diminished. "Tit for tat" is severely faulty thinking.

We are duty-bound to assist our male counterparts as we traverse this road into the last quarter of our lives. Why you ask? Because, it's what we do. Even if you do not know a single man in your life, wish them well. Wish all beings and creatures well. This life can be uncertain, and we do not know what the grumpy person behind us in line at the checkout has been through. Maybe they are grumpy because something terrible happened to them? I believe many of us are quick to condemn men, especially if we are lacking in positive relationships with men, for all the problems in our society. But it's not them; it's the few villains in power pulling the strings. While being a woman in this world is no picnic, being a man is hard too.

Senior citizens have the highest rate of suicide. Men are far more likely to succeed in their attempts, and let's also look at who is responsible for most mass murders in America - men. I'm not going to get into gun control issues. A gun is a tool, plain and simple. It does not pull its own trigger. That is a person, often men, pulling that trigger. Why, is the question, and how do we thwart such things? Maybe with loving kindness. Since we or a loved one could end up in the cross-hairs of some angry gunman, let's work to have fewer angry people out there. One way to do that is with guidance and care.

There is no shame in moving from the warrior to the next role in life. There is no embarrassment in bodily changes. Most people have not achieved all of their goals in life at age 50. Many of us have had so many twists and turns on the road of life we can barely understand some of the paths we found ourselves on over the years. Shaming men for these things, when we ourselves are looking for understanding, serves no one. It's the same prejudice that has us living in subjugation and unable to reach as high as we'd like. While we have glass ceilings, men have the provider legacy. It's weighty in its own way.

The more we can lead the way, encourage the next step on this ladder of life, and offer understanding and kinship to our brethren, the more we can tamp down domestic violence, mass violence, and men's fears which often comes out in violent, ego-maniacal, and ruthless ways. Moving into being the orca is the natural way. Moving from warrior to wise man is equally vital. We are all vital, and we all have our roles as we traverse this life. We need to embrace them, and encourage all of us to embrace exactly where we are at this moment. Are you a global citizen, or a selfish bitch? Choose ye well, the history of the world depends on it!

Tell the men that at different times in life we are different people. Embrace your step up to Chief, Shaman, Wise-man, or Elder. You were not meant to be a Warrior forever. Embrace the beauty of this journey. If you need a sports car or a young lover, or just a different lover, you should go get it! Maybe you need to learn something new. Open your mind to experiences. Embrace the ride. Enjoy stepping off the battlefield -- where there is only action and little thought. Embrace peace. Peace within, and peace without.

ARE YOU LEAVING MORE THAN JUST A STAIN?

That is a shitty question, I know, but I am asking it seriously. I ask it of myself every day. How much TV do you watch? How much social media scrolling? How much toiling on nonsense? We complain about the kids today, but we are the same. We are teaching them that behavior. All of us staring into our palms. I get your knees might hurt, mine too, but what are we doing to take in the beauty around us, to share that beauty, and to honor this world now?

Yeah, it sounds like idealism. We need more idealism, not less. More altruism, kindness, and generosity. If we have never had time for idealism in our lives before, why not now? If not now, then when? I want to leave this place better than I found it. It's been turning quickly into a shit-hole my entire life. I was taught to be a nihilist as a kid growing up in the 1980s. I was taught it was hopeless. I watched the birth of the rust belt when the steel mills all closed. I remember when President Reagan moved the doomsday clock to two minutes to midnight, as the USSR collapsed. Iron Maiden wrote a song about it.

My parents paid off their house in the mid-1980s, a house they bought for $14,000 in 1969. That's probably what my father earned in a year at the fire department. I owe more than $200,000 on my rustic cottage and I'm nearly 55. That used to be the age of retirement, at least in America's brief golden era it was. Now most people my age figure they will die on the job.

I have marched in the street and carried a sign before. It felt kind of futile, but I see the importance of it too. In 1991, in a march against the first Gulf War, Chicago police led us all surprisingly onto Lake Shore Drive. The protest stopped traffic for a good few hours, well into rush hour. At the time we saw it as some kind of win. Years later, I realized it was the city's move to make every inconvenienced commuter hate our guts. Divide and conquer, every step of the way!

No way am I calling marching, or taking to the streets, useless. Sometimes it is our duty. It is up to us to stand firm. I learned a lot about successful protest from living in the Pacific Northwest. Early on after landing here, I learned that protests organized through some of the amazing community radio people and other activists stopped the building of a nuclear power plant on a dangerous fault-line. While living there, they successfully stopped a Liquid Natural Gas (LNG) refinery from building on the vital estuary at the mouth of the Columbia River. The LNG company tried every dirty trick to get a permit to build their giant hub, and time and time again organized protest, in a variety of media, brought enough awareness to successfully fight it. A rare victory! Bravo!

All lot of those people are in their 70s and 80s or dead. Who is stepping up? Punk bands from the 1980s are still having to stand up. Noam Chomsky is still having to stand up. It's maybe time we all stand up. For something. Not fanatically, but with strength and truth.

I don't do enough. I have stood in the street when it was needed, when I could. I have volunteered in a number of capacities over the years. I have tried to communicate to people and share things that seem important. I have stood up for free speech, for better and for worse. I've created art. In my personal life, I've tried to help friends and acquaintances when they have asked, or I try to offer help to those in need, but I could do more.

Am I leaving more than a stain on the sofa or chair or my bedsheets? I sure want to. This is part of it for me, I guess, this little book of personal pep talks. I am saying all this to myself really. You are just here for it. I'm sharing my own struggles and epiphanies as I reach this point in life. Maybe it will help others, or it will help us find camaraderie in this quest to leave the world better than we found it.

One of the biggest problems facing the world today is not so much "climate change" as the media calls it, but the poisoning of the land, the water, and the air. It's no joke.

Pollution.

We create so much waste. We waste so much, from freezer burned meat to never eaten leftovers. From disposable diapers to tires to the clear plastic cases every pastry you buy or pint of berries or that laundry detergent comes ensconced in. Why do we use plastic berry containers once? Why are our pastries and everything else wrapped in plastic? Why don't we refill containers? Why don't we all have bidets on our toilets? I feel like a heathen using toilet paper made from trees. Think about using all those disposable tampons and pads. How much plastic from shampoo bottles have I created in my lifetime? It's ponderous and onerous.

If I think about it, I am ashamed. But it's not me, it is the system. The system. If it doesn't work, why continue?

Save all the plastic you or your family uses in a month. Do it as an experiment. I saved all of my plastic for a month; it was brutal. I still have it. I still do it now. I try to reuse everything, and I think a lot more about what I buy from the store. I won't buy berries in a plastic clam shell if I can help it. I try to go to bakeries where they put their stuff in boxes. Would it be better if their box was made of hemp or bamboo? Yeah it would, but that needs to come. Maybe from you? We need to be more thoughtful about wood, about throwing things away, about what we are doing and how much waste we are creating.

Even if you are a master recycler, even if you never litter, is that really enough? Most of us just throw that stuff away. Into the recycling, right? Beyond the lack of actual recycling. Recycling itself, things like melting plastics again and again, are still poisoning the air, water, and soil.

From my own personal experience of working in a plastic factory for five years in the early 1990s, here's what I know about plastic recycling: We would get 2500 pound gaylord boxes of shredded plastic to test for recycling at our plant. They came on wooden pallets by the truckload. The gaylord boxes were the size of the pallet and the same in height. The shredded plastic looked like confetti. My job was to test it to make sure different plastics were not mixed together - Polystyrene and polypropylene are different from high or low density polyethylene. All have different melt temperatures. If other plastics were mixed into the ton of shredded plastics - easily discernible by pressing a sample between two heated thin metal plates - the entire truckload went to the landfill. This melt test was part of my job in the quality control lab.

We made color concentrate for plastic products, everything from vacuum cleaners to car parts to the blue white shade of Styrofoam cups. It was a good job for someone like me. I earned almost $10 an hour. I had medical and dental insurance that was okay. I had paid federal holidays, overtime pay for anything over eight hours in a day or 40 hours in a week, sick days, and two weeks paid vacation. The downside was it was toxic.

Every six months, a bus would come to test our blood. All of us, maybe 125 people who worked in the plastic factory. It wasn't to see if we were on drugs - most of us were, mostly weed which was illegal then, and a couple guys smoked crack. The Mexican guys mostly drank Budweiser, most of them didn't smoke weed. The poor white guys were the guys on crack. Everyone was "good people" -- the guys on crack, the ex-cons, the Mexican and Central American guys who came here long ago on perilous routes.

On my shift, four to midnight, it was maybe a dozen guys, plus the foreman, and me in the lab. I tested the pellets we extruded on the lines every hour, and ran tests to make sure they were concentrated enough. I matched the colors that were going to be next on the line. We all worked hard. Our goal was the best color concentrate we could create. But, there was a ton of waste, "just the way it was", we were told. It bothered every one of us. We often made weird art out of the scrap to feel like we were using it for something. That waste was not including those 2500 pound gaylord boxes of recycling that went to the dump.

We used dangerous pigments, which is the reason why the bus actually came to check our blood. They tested our lead and zinc levels. If blood levels got too high with lead or zinc, the worker would be removed for a period of time. It was over 100 degrees on the third floor of the factory in the summers. The guys didn't want to wear the respirators. They were breathing millions of particles of powdered pigment, lead, cadmium, iron, and titanium.

The factory was over a hundred years old. It sat in the center of a wetlands, along the Little Calumet River. On the other side of the river was a range of mountainous toxic landfills, and next to us was an adhesives factory. I worked there five years. My old work buddy Jose tells me it recently closed. We keep in touch on Facebook. His father and brother worked there too, but they have both since passed.

I realize I'm getting off on a tangent, but am I?

Plastic factories. Disposable everything. Poorly constructed buildings that grow black mold. Destruction of nature for senseless progress. Destroying wetlands, marshes, forests, and mountains for shoddy subdivisions and apartment complexes, when so many homes sit vacant. Strip malls built only to stand only a few decades while destroying a millennia of a meadow.

What it comes down to is that bottom line world. When everything is based on "the bottom line", the bottom is where we land. Houses used to be built by craftsmen. Office buildings and stores were built to be beautiful. Today, stores are merely steel squares built as cheaply as possible with lousy supplies, poor design, using low level labor instead of skilled artisans and experts. Strip malls are made to come down in 20 years, rather than creating something well-planned and beautiful, something to last centuries, and that raises our souls when we see it.

Pardon me: I grew up in Chicago, where godly visionaries sought to create beauty out of ashes and rubble. They didn't want to destroy beauty with steel box shopping and mitigated wetlands on ten percent of the land. No. Men like Louis Sullivan and Daniel Burnham, and Marshall Field, and Potter and Bertha Palmer, and Al Capone (yes, Al Capone), all worked to build a beautiful city. They had foresight. They helped to create masterful structures, buildings with perfect sound, loaded with artistic design -- to add to the majesty of the city the best that they could -- not the dollar store version of America that has been created since the 1980s. When we offer the lowest quality stuff into the world, we destroy ourselves. We destroy the future.

When I look to my parents and ask smugly "What did my parents do to make the world better in their lifetimes?" I personally am met with staggering piles of heroics. I feel like anything I have done, or could do, pales in comparison to the two of them. I have big shoes to step into. My parents gave their lives to others. They were also flawed human beings, no one is perfect. They were amazing in so many more ways than their falters. We all falter.

My father carried people from burning buildings for 28 years. He saved lives, he put out fires, and he cooked for his men. He broke a few bones. Once he had carbon monoxide poisoning because he kept running in to save elderly people from a nursing home fire. He was air lifted by helicopter to a hospital on the other side of the city where there was a chamber to detox from the smoke. He received a plaque from the city in a special ceremony when I was a kid. My dad was a hero.

My father was part of the proud brotherhood of professional firemen. I can say that because it was then. There were no female firemen in the 1960s or early '70s. In fact, my father was the training officer who performed the agility tests for all prospective firefighters. He tested and put forward the city's first female and first black firefighters for the team in Calumet City. We were poor.

He also did side work; all firemen had second jobs. My father was a master tuckpointer, repairing masonry work on old buildings in the summers, and he hung drywall and finished walls in the winters. I was so lucky to work for him as a laborer from around 11 to 18 years old, I learned skills that I have put to use on my places of residence for decades! Stocky & Daughters.

My mother devoted her life, as both a volunteer and a professional librarian, to sharing her love of books with children. Children loved her for it. I loved her for teaching me to read at three years old. She became a volunteer librarian at a parochial school even though she loathed organized religion. There was a need and she did it. Later, she was hired on at the public elementary school as the afternoon librarian where she worked for probably over 20 years.

My mother and the woman who worked as the morning librarian were much cheaper than Mrs. Turner, the full-time, master degreed librarian, who in the pared down Reaganomics of Education got pushed to be an English teacher "if she wanted to keep her job".

My mother worked to be the best librarian she could. The children would always be excited to see us out or happen upon our house on Halloween. "Mrs. Stocky!" They would exclaim with delight in their voices. It made me proud as a kid, even as a teenage stoner. My parents were beautiful human beings. Of course they were not perfect, no one is, but they spent their entire lives putting good forward. Real good, not bullshit good or religious garbage. They were never self-righteous. How does one top that? I can never be as great as my parents.

I was 10 years old or so when Ronald Reagan was elected president. I experienced first-hand the gutting of our education system. No more music teacher, no more art supplies, no more librarian. When I got to high school in Reagan's second term in office, I never once got to check a book out of my high school library because they had no librarian, and not even someone part-time, no volunteers. It was dark and locked for the entire four years I attended high school. Occasionally we attended class inside the library or a special meeting of some sort, but we could never check out a book. Reaganomics!

But I digress. What I am talking about here is doing the best we can in some part of our life to make the world a better place, to help others, to improve life. For me, the issue of plastic and pollution is a big one. Where I grew up it was a wasteland. They call it the Rust Belt, but it was so much more than steel.

The oil refinery puts billions of gallons of waste into Lake Michigan and Wolf Lake. The Calumet River was completely dead for years, not a single fish, nothing. It was front page news in the Hammond Times, the local Calumet Region newspaper, when sludge-worms were found to survive in the polluted water. It sounds like I am exaggerating, but I'm not. If you grew up in a different place, you just can't understand. No one would dare eat the fish out of the Calumet River. Not out of Wolf Lake either.

My father used to catch crayfish in Wolf Lake for bait in Minnesota. And in more bizarreness, I learned that the lakes in Minnesota are stocked by the government because all the weekend fishing did the native populations in. Stocked lakes. Think of the concept of that.

Think about all the stories of children having to drink beer and wine in the old country because the water wasn't fit to drink. When my old friend Heart Warrior Chosa ran for Governor of Minnesota, part of her platform was that "shitting in water is a dirty habit from the old country." I had never thought about it before that!

She said the Ojibwe moved in the winter instead of staying and chopping all of the trees down for survival. I'm not suggesting we all go "van life". What I am suggesting is maybe solar. Maybe buried power lines. In the 1950s scientists were speaking of hydrogen as "the power of the future". Now inventors are looking at it again. Farms used to all have windmills, and they did more than tell us which way the wind was blowing. They powered machines that made grain into flour, ran water, or made heat.

Today, we are so removed from the family farm, they barely exist. It's all suburban sprawl where barns and fields of wheat or corn or whatever else grew, with a farmhouse in the distance. Now we have apartment complexes. I can remember farms right by us growing up, at the edges of the city. Squash, melons, berries, only a few minutes away. It all became houses, and ugly houses at that.

There are so many ills in society. If you as a person do what you can to help with just one, imagine the impact it could have in the world! Imagine if we got together on things we agree on, how powerful we could be! All our pods of orcas joining together to flip yachts and stop the destruction of our world. What a concept!

What if we said we don't want cheaply made housing, built by workers with low skills, earning poor wages? Let's as a society teach our youth as much as we can from building skills to Shakespeare and see where their interests land. In the Bottom Line Economy, school books of today are poorly written and uninformed. Have you ever seen a high school science textbook from the 1950s? College graduates today probably couldn't understand it. Here in America knowledge is kept from us, locked up like my high school library. Our educational system could be robust instead of stagnant. No more can we let political agendas and corporations run our schools and colleges.

Be like the orca; lead the way. If you were the person who always made the wrong decision in life, if you often let yourself down, you can change that in this fourth quarter. Find your way forward, and figure out what you can offer in lessons from your mistakes. Failing teaches so much! Teach from that. If you have a special skill or passion you never tapped into because it was considered weird or "no way to earn a living", now is the time to experiment. Who knows what you have to teach us.

They want us to question if the planet is flat. They want to bring young people into the fearful darkness of religious fervor. It's evident watching social media. Young people are taught nothing today. Ask a high school student who their favorite poet is. They don't know any poets. Do you? Can you recite a single poem?

My grandparents on my mother's side fell in love over a shared love of Henry Wadsworth Longfellow, and I've been told they would often recite passages of his work to each other. They were eighteen or nineteen then. How many people that age can recite Longfellow? Do they even know who he is? Can they recite any poem? Are they even taught about poetry today? It seems all the beauty of learning has been removed from school. This system needs us dumb, it needs us nihilistic, and it needs our apathy and division.

If we don't stop the spiral of stupidity in America today, we have only ourselves to blame. We need to teach the youth. We need to learn too.

Today we can stop being part of the status quo. We can stop the cycles of sorrow that we pass generationally. Everyone messes up as a parent, as a child of a parent, as a human. We all fail. We can turn it around.

Be the orca! Take the lead and do something to make your community better. Do you know your neighbors? Do you know your local politicians? I'm not talking about politics or parties here. I'm talking about asking questions and demanding better.

We want real food. We want natural fiber clothing. We want to eat fish from our rivers. We want true education, open to all. We want to see a doctor when we need to. We want to have libraries and parks and fresh air and clean water. We don't want miles of tire fires, and no one should be sleeping on the streets or homeless. Even the condemned man has a bed and a roof. No more war machine. The people of every nation, the orcas of every land say no more!

The orca takes the lead. She takes the reins and her rightful place leading her pod. I get it, I am throwing a lot at you in this final urging. Certainly, I am urging you. I am begging you. Woman. Take the lead.

How are we being more than a stain on the sofa? Sometimes taking care of ourselves is all we can muster. Life is hard. I understand. Sometimes we are called to do more. I say this change of life is what we make it. Don't be desensitized to the wrongs around you. It is not hopeless. There is work to be done! Follow your heart, follow your instincts, follow what you know is right. Lead, teach, help, serve. Be the orca!

IN CONCLUSiON

There was so much I wanted to say here. I'm sure I didn't say everything I had hoped to, but this is what I could capture on the page. The best words certainly left in my dreams. According to my notes, I began to write these thoughts just about two years ago. There have been many stops and starts, lost writings that I'll likely find six months from now, fears that needed to be faced, and so many struggles. I persevered to see it through.

I have concerns I may sound crazy; I guess I am. I have concerns I may sound traumatized; I'm sure I do. I fear I offered too much personal information; I'm sure I did. But here is my manifesto, for myself, for what I want the rest of my life to be about.

The ideas inside this small volume are what I am striving for. I have come a long way in the years since my 50th birthday, but there is further to go. I have come to accept myself, and not just that: I love myself today. I truly accept myself. Perhaps more than I ever have. I have come through some dark nights of the soul. I have healed. I have grieved. I have experienced life in so many ways. I have been in dire straits, and I have felt on top of the world - sometimes at the same time!

I have no idea what comes after we take our last breath and leave this vessel. It could be nothingness, or it could be amazing. That day will come, but I will not spend my time thinking about it. This manifesto has nothing to do with penance or doing good for some false entitlement in the next realm.

Merely, I want to offer something to hopefully leave This World better than I found it in some small way. Every musician, every artist and writer, every naturalist, every farmer, we all want to leave this world better than we found it. I'm not a professional hero like my parents. This is what I can do.

Thank you for taking time with this tome, I hope something in it helped you. I hope you will seek out ways to "Be the Orca" in your community, family, and/or life.

Well Wishes & Love,
Amy E Stocky

ACKNOWLEDGMENTS

I am so thankful for all of the amazing women I have known. Thank you for being part of my life!

These are just some of the remarkable women who have had an effect on my life and my being:

Mary Joan O'Hearn
Francine O'Hearn
Margaret O'Hearn
April Stocky
Sarah Decrescenzo
Aunt Marci
Pat McCallum
Aunt Verna
Miss Gates
Gwen and Mamie
Loretta Jambic
Marie Tharp
Heart Warrior Chosa
Anne Stewart
Jimella Lucas
Nanci Main
Shirley Keifor
Lark Ryan
Nikki and Dianne Hackborn
Zoreh Mohammadzadeh
Carol Newman
Wenda Vorce
Jane Herrold
Lani Jo Leigh
Carol Baldwin
Jonnel Fowler
Lois Eisenhower
Helen Kagin
Pat Jolly
Jessie Nurkowski
Shauna Lynch
Khristina Smith
Ugly Shyla & Darlene Munster
Rachel Kieserman
Neveah Rorbach
Sandra Pearson
Jen Reed
Peg Davis
Lindsay Bones
Roxanne
Myrtle
Cheyenne
Lucy
Sasha, Cookie, & Susie

Betty Ondreyka
Mary Ann Carrol
Miriam Atkins
Crimson Crutchfield
Christine Snider
Amanda Metcalfe
Lori Beth Bravo
Sarah Kandiko
Madeline Pointer
Julie & Wendy
Roxanne & Nicole
Jan Bono
Debra Orzel
Tammy Crutchfield
Belinda Emanuel
Fordinka Kanlic
Phaedra Bonewits
Amy Samples
Rachel Golston
Miranda Rinks
Elleda Wilson
Pamalot Roberts
Ivy Nelson
Mrs. Gish
Ursula Pachuki
Miss Krance
Mrs. Randulich
Miss Della
Mrs. Zygmunt
Mrs. Turner
Rhi Dennison
Marly Preston
Season Cole
Theresa Reed
Tammy Lanham
Annette LaRue
Amy Bean
Hobie Bender
Linda & Stephanie Conard
Starlyn Chavez
Thandi Rosenbaum
Paula Scarcelli
Deborah Purdy Pamplin
And so many more!

www.ingramcontent.com/pod-product-compliance
Lightning Source LLC
Chambersburg PA
CBHW072200070526
44585CB00015B/1232